METAMORPHOSES

METAMORPHOSES

IN SEARCH OF FRANZ KAFKA

KAROLINA WATROBA

PEGASUS BOOKS

NEW YORK LONDON

METAMORPHOSES

Pegasus Books, Ltd.
148 West 37th Street, 13th Floor
New York, NY 10018

First Pegasus Books cloth edition June 2024

ISBN: 978-1-63936-671-2

10 9 8 7 6 5 4 3 2 1

Printed in the United States of America
Distributed by Simon & Schuster
www.pegasusbooks.com

Contents

PROLOGUE

What Makes Kafka Kafka

Franz Kafka's life is both very easy and very difficult to summarise. Easy because it was short – he was born in 1883 and died in 1924, and so lived forty years, give or take; spent mostly in one place – central Prague; and one job – in the field of insurance law. His health was poor; he never married or started a family; did not travel much, and never outside of Europe; did not go to war. But then in other ways Kafka's life cannot be recapitulated so easily. Our commonplace ideas about national, ethnic, religious and linguistic identity, for example, cannot do justice to him, which is why he seems to be called something different in every biographical blurb you might come across – German, Austrian, Czech, Jewish and various combinations of the above. Despite his bachelordom, largely spent in Prague, he managed to develop significant relationships with four women from four different cities in four different countries. He also often fantasised about travelling or even moving permanently, and was keen on learning about other places and cultures, which gave his life a much broader intellectual horizon than might appear at first glance.

Besides, however mundane many of his life's events might have been, Kafka kept track of them in numerous notebooks, diaries and letters, of which many thousands of pages have survived. A record of conflicts with his family, especially with his father; of friendships; of books he read, plays he went to, languages he learnt, dreams he had, food he ate; his ailments, fears, anxieties, hopes, the things he enjoyed; the things he said or did to other people, both kind and unkind. This, combined with the almost unimaginable wealth of scholarship that has investigated, and continues to investigate, virtually every facet of his life, from distant cousins to sexual escapades, and from digestive issues to the brand of hairbrush he used, gives us an uncommonly comprehensive insight into the life of this man who died one hundred years ago.

Such is the depth and breadth of our collective obsession with this Kafka, however, that we do not often stop to think *why* it is that we are so interested in him. The answer might seem obvious. In his notebooks, scattered in between entries about what his boss said at work and where he went for an evening walk, Kafka wrote down numerous stories and literary fragments, including three unfinished novels. *The Metamorphosis, The Judgement, The Trial, The Castle*: these are among the most famous, the most recognisable works of Kafka, but also of the twentieth century, of the German literary canon – perhaps of the whole of world literature, across history. Some of these works were published in his lifetime; most were not. Some of the relatively few early readers who encountered his works as he was writing them – the vast majority in the ten years between 1912 and 1922, when he was in his thirties – were deeply impressed. Chief among them was his best friend and later first editor Max Brod, from early on possessed of an unshakeable belief in Franz Kafka's literary genius.

It might seem obvious, then, where our obsession with Kafka's life stems from, what animates his countless biographies. We want to know what made Kafka Kafka. But while the cultural environment, historical context and personal experiences that shaped his life did influence Kafka's writing in myriad ways – as we shall see in the pages that follow – there is also another part to this story, a part that does not get told nearly as often. To understand how Kafka became Kafka, we cannot stop in 1924, the year of his death, where most biographies end. To gain the status he eventually gained, Kafka needed readers. Readers who would share Brod's belief in his extraordinary gifts. Almost all these readers only got their hands on his books after his death, many in translation. How did it happen? Who were some of those readers and how did they impact his literary fame? Why have Kafka's writings resonated with so many people, in so many places, at so many points in time? Why do we keep reading him today? And what might we learn about literature, and about ourselves, the species that cares so much about it, by telling Kafka's story in this way – through the stories of his readers around the world, over the past century?

To answer these questions, I travelled across time and space in the footsteps of dozens of Kafka's readers: from a British aristocrat-turned-scholar poring over Kafka's writings in the bowels of a Swiss bank vault to ordinary readers from all corners of the globe leaving notes at Kafka's grave in Prague, and from a war veteran in Berlin who survived life in the trenches but feels defeated by the newly published, enigmatic tale of *The Metamorphosis* to a hip Korean writer transforming the Kafkaesque into a Man Booker International Prize-winning feminist manifesto a century later.

In the process, I approached my guiding question – what made Kafka Kafka? – from many different angles. For one thing, it has certainly helped that he was a well-educated European man who wrote in German, a language with many speakers and much cultural prestige. All this meant that, despite the very real prejudices he faced as a Jewish person, his books still had a relative advantage in reaching a wide readership: he was able to access publication venues, translation networks and cultural circles with an international reach that popularised his works, both before and after his death. Many examples of such 'technologies of recognition', to use literary theorist Shu-mei Shih's term, were at work during Kafka's life and afterlife, and are discussed in the chapters to come.

But many other well-educated, European, German-speaking men produced copious amounts of writing over the centuries too and yet never achieved the kind of global recognition that Kafka did. Some of this was due to sheer serendipity. In Chapters One and Two, I recount the story of Kafka's various manuscripts: some were burnt, lost or confiscated; others *nearly* burnt, lost or confiscated. The fate of those papers was often down to the decisions and actions of individuals. Other kinds of serendipity were at play too. The name 'Kafka', with its brevity, pleasing symmetry and ease of pronunciation in many languages, not to mention a rather attractive meaning in Czech, turned out to be an unexpected marketing boon at various points in Kafka's lifetime and beyond, as we shall see in Chapters Three and Five. His name has even given rise to a popular adjective, used everywhere from back-cover blurbs of innumerable literary fiction books to the pages of the *Daily Mail*, examples of which are discussed in Chapter Four and sprinkled through-out the book.

But what about the intrinsic aesthetic value of his works, you might ask at this point? It was important, of course – but perhaps not exactly in the way one might expect. As we shall see, many of Kafka's early readers, even highly skilled literary critics and well-educated German-speaking Jews who shared much of Kafka's background, were puzzled by his works. Some found them difficult and frustrating; others compared them to books by contemporary authors, many of whom are today almost entirely forgotten. Given this context, it would be difficult to claim that Kafka's works heralded the arrival of an absolutely novel, objectively unique and universally compelling literary quality. And yet over time, as the literature of the early twentieth century – the literature of modernity – became history, Kafka was elevated to the status of one of its patron saints, alongside the likes of Joyce, Proust and Woolf. I address Kafka's status as a modernist icon and show in detail the workings of his literary technique at various points in this book.

But to proclaim the aesthetic value of a piece of writing is a strangely unsatisfactory, theoretical exercise. To experi-ence it in practice is not only infinitely more enjoyable – it is also the foundation of any compelling theory. That is why throughout this book I do not just explain what Kafka's writings are about and what they are like, but also show what they have meant to various readers, often very differ-ent than me. For once the more tangible factors – Kafka's social position; the happy accidents that helped his works along; the mechanisms by which literary canons are formed; the distinctive characteristics of his writing – are explained and accounted for, there is still something left to explore. A reader and a book: the alchemy of an encounter. *Metamorphoses: In Search of Franz Kafka* is ultimately about why Kafka matters – and, more broadly, what literature does to us, and for us.

Kafka himself was well aware of this mysterious power that books and writers can wield over their readers. Throughout his life, he had a knack for startling, pithy, aphoristic pronouncements, even if they had to be painfully coaxed out of the agony of writer's block. Brod would later claim that Kafka never wrote a 'single line', not a 'single word', not even when briefly jotting down a casual little note for a friend, that was not 'infused with a special magic charm'. This is clearly an exaggeration – but plenty of such one-liners can be found, also on the topic of reading. In 1903, twenty-year-old Kafka writes to a friend: 'Some books seem like a key to unfamiliar rooms in one's own castle.' He was reading the medieval mystic Meister Eckhart at the time. A year later: 'A book must be the axe for the frozen sea inside us.' This time he was engrossed in the diaries of Friedrich Hebbel, a nineteenth-century dramatist. And then in 1915, Kafka writes in his diary of the Swedish playwright August Strindberg: 'I'm not reading him to read him, but to lie on his chest.'

Whether knowingly or not, over the years many a reader has taken a cue from the man himself and developed attachments to Kafka's writing of the kind that he imagined in some of his own most precious moments as a reader. Kafka's books have acted as a point of access for the exploration of the hidden corners of many readers' sense of self – 'a key to unfamiliar rooms in one's own castle'; as a tool for a startling, violent rupture in their unthinking or unfeeling existence – 'the axe for the frozen sea inside us'; and as an intimate, nurturing embrace – the breast at which to lie. Let us meet some of those readers now, and let them guide our exploration of Kafka's work, life and afterlife.

1

Oxford

English Kafka

Migrations

The other night I was having dinner with colleagues and ended up talking to a visiting professor of medieval history from the United States. She asked what I was working on. A book on Franz Kafka, I said. She knew who he was: a fantastically influential writer, a German-speaking Jew who had lived in largely Czech-speaking Prague one hundred years ago, the author of modernist classics like *The Trial*, *The Castle* and *The Metamorphosis*, often described as atmospheric, enigmatic books about inscrutable bureaucrats, mysterious courts and entrapped protagonists with names like 'Josef K.' or just 'K.'.

I am trying to get closer to understanding Kafka through the stories of his readers, I explained to my dinner companion. How fascinating, she answered; she had taken a class on Kafka in college and loved his writing. There was one thing I should make sure to explain in my book, though, she immediately added, namely how *funny* Kafka is: people take him too seriously, she thought. They miss the satirical, dark, self-deprecating humour of Central European Jews at the turn of the twentieth century. She could see it because she was brought up with it: both of her parents' families were Central European Jews who had fled Nazi persecution to the United States. In fact, she added somewhat diffidently, did I know that she was herself distantly related to Kafka? Her great-grandmother's sister-in-law was Kafka's second cousin – close enough to have gone to his funeral, almost exactly a century ago.

There I was, eating mushroom risotto in the dining room of an Oxford college next to a woman whose relatives had been to Kafka's funeral one hundred years ago. Rarely had I felt closer to him – and to the mysterious workings of cultural affinity. Books have the power to stir us and to connect us in unexpected ways. For my dinner companion, Kafka's works captured and preserved the oblique humour central to how she thought about her own family – its history and survival in the face of the great catastrophes of the twentieth century. For me, Kafka was quickly becoming a strange obsession.

At first, it seemed like a perfectly ordinary interest for a scholar of German literature. Kafka was one of the most famous German-language writers of all time, if not *the* most famous, after all. And yet my connection to him felt special. I was not Jewish but, had I been born in his times, Kafka and I would have been compatriots. Like Prague, in the nineteenth and early twentieth century my hometown of Cracow lay on the northern edge of the Austro-Hungarian Empire. I was born more than one hundred years after him, long after the dissolution of the Habsburg Empire – and yet we still ended up as neighbours: I now live and work in Oxford, right next to the Bodleian Library, which houses most of Kafka's surviving manuscripts. In post-Brexit Britain, with all the talk of making Britain great again, hostility against immigrants and non-dominant ethnicities and religious groups, and the government de-prioritising the teaching of foreign languages and cultures in schools and at universities, it is hard to shake the feeling that neither of us makes too much sense here.

This book is my attempt to shake this feeling once and for all, by showing how we can write cultural history in a way that includes rather than excludes, how we can put interactions and overlaps between cultures front and centre rather than painting a picture of separate and disjointed national trajectories, and how we can pay attention to the ways in which books from faraway times and places come alive in the hands of individual readers. The way we think about the history of literature changes if we start thinking of books and their authors as belonging to readers rather than nations – beyond the boundaries of space, time and language.

For one thing, it gives me licence not to begin this book by telling you about Kafka's birth in the summer of 1883 in Prague. I will eventually get to Prague in a later chapter, but first let me explain why I do not think we can – or should – jump straight into Kafka's life. In the model of literary history that I want to share, which scholars sometimes refer to as the study of reception, reading is always a relationship between a book and its reader. The reader must first reflect on her own position and identity because otherwise her unexamined assumptions and previous experiences – of both life and literature – can cloud her relationship with the book. But this does not mean that the reader's identity is an obstacle to her engagement with the book. As we will see time and time again, and as we have already seen with my dinner companion, a serious appraisal of where readers are coming from – both literally and figuratively – can help us see with much more clarity why and how books matter.

I begin as I must – right where I am, with a neat row of Kafka's books stretching out on the shelf behind me: my study in Oxford, ten years almost to the day after I first arrived here from Cracow, a Polish city some 250 miles to the east of Prague.

With all the eagerness of a newly minted student and immigrant, I quickly filled up my calendar with the academic events on offer that October. The largest one was held at the Sheldonian Theatre, where I had just matriculated as a first-year student of German literature. Oxford was celebrating the joint purchase – with the German Literature Archive in Marbach – of a collection of letters and postcards that Franz had written to his favourite sister, Ottilie, known as Ottla. A specialist lecture and a reading from *Kafka's Dick*, Alan Bennett's irreverent play in which Kafka pays a visit to a Yorkshire couple, accompanied an exhibition of the newly acquired letters. Other Kafka manuscripts owned by the Bodleian Library were on display too: two of his three novels, *The Man who Disappeared* (also known as *America*) and *The Castle*, as well as *The Metamorphosis*, Kafka's most famous story, which was one of my set texts that year.

As I walked under the Bridge of Sighs on a crisp autumn morning, my own copy of *The Metamorphosis* in hand, on my way to steal a peek at those treasured manuscripts through a glass case in one of the largest and oldest libraries in the world, I had many questions. How had I, a Polish teenager with a love for books and foreign languages, but without any connections in England, ended up here? And more importantly: how did the manuscripts of some of the most famous books of the twentieth century, penned by Kafka in German, in Prague, not far from where I came from, and also bearing no obvious connection to England, end up here? In other words: why did Oxford have so many of Kafka's manuscripts? And why exactly did people expend so much attention – and money – on old pieces of paper, when anybody who actually wanted to read the thing could buy a perfectly usable modern edition? This reverence for old objects that had once belonged to somebody important smacked of the devotion with which believers approached religious relics and, since I had just revolted against the Catholic Church, this was bound to rub me up the wrong way.

What was already clear at the time, though, was that Kafka's writing was indeed very special, unlike anything I had ever read before. Its magnetic force, its mysterious hold over so many readers, was apparent as I took in the large audience gathered at the Sheldonian. Generations of scholars and critics had pored over the question of what makes Kafka unique, and yet – as with all great writers – they did not seem to have exhausted it. It has taken me some time, but now – a decade later, and after many hours of puzzling over Kafka's dreamlike texts under Oxford's dreaming spires – I am ready to circle back to this question, and to that special day in the Sheldonian.

Locked Out of the Library

Over the years I have found that the best way to understand a writer is to understand his readers. As the centenary of Kafka's death in 1924 draws nearer, readers all over the world will reach for his books again, or for the first time. I want to meet them – and not just academics. I want to find books, films and plays in various languages that rewrite Kafka for the twenty-first century, just as Alan Bennett did with *Kafka's Dick* in the 1980s. I want to listen in as book clubs discuss his texts, to read reviews on personal blogs, visit museums that tell Kafka's story a century after his death and read notes left at his grave in Prague by his readers.

I concoct this plan at the beginning of 2020. But we all know what comes next: the global Covid-19 pandemic. For more than a year, I will not leave Oxford at all. I am here, in the very spot where I first found myself thinking about Kafka's writings. But, in a rather Kafkaesque turn of events, when I decide that it is time for me to go to the Bodleian to examine Kafka's fabled manuscripts up close for the first time in my decade at Oxford, we enter a national lockdown. The library gates shut. I am not allowed to enter.

Fortunately, I do not live in one of Kafka's nightmarish tales, and 2020 soon teaches us that we can find new ways of accessing things that seem inaccessible. At the end of March, the Bodleian hosts a webinar about museum conservation and Kafka's manuscripts. I sign up and soon am sitting in front of my laptop, just one individual in an audience of a few hundred, looking at high-resolution photos of Kafka's manuscripts, and listening to Fiona McLees, the conservator who has been working on these 'celebrity items', as she calls them, for the past few years. We find out that only two or three people a year are granted access to the manuscripts, and that in fact the library does not receive many more requests to see them. Regardless, the curators lavish loving care on the manuscripts in an effort to preserve the frail paper of the inconspicuous octavo and quarto notebooks that Kafka often used for his writing, and other bundles of handwritten pages.

As I listen to McLees, I am struck by one point in particular: she does not know German, so cannot read the manuscripts herself, and yet her working life is devoted to ensuring that these papers survive. How oddly appropriate for a writer seen by many as the symbol of literary inscrutability, the writer of enigmas: the one person whose job it is to look at his manuscripts literally cannot read them.

In her talk, McLees quotes extensively from a paper by Philip Larkin, here in his capacity as a librarian rather than poet. One of Larkin's terms that McLees is particularly interested in is the 'magical value' of a manuscript. 'All literary manuscripts have two kinds of value: what might be called the magical value and the meaningful value', Larkin said in a paper given to the Manuscripts Group of the Standing Conference of National and University Libraries in 1979. 'The magical value is the older and more universal: this is the paper [the writer] wrote on, these are the words as he wrote them, emerging for the first time in this particular miraculous combination.'

As McLees puts it, 'Handling the manuscripts so intimately gives you a – perhaps imagined – sense of the person who produced them.' It seems to bring us closer to the mystery of literary creation. I was not so far off after all when I thought, seeing the Kafka manuscripts for the first time, that they were being displayed like religious relics. It has long been argued that in the twentieth century art became a form of secular religion. Readers may value manuscripts the same way Catholics value relics of saints. In fact, McLees herself does not shy away from using the language of religion when talking about the manuscripts. She describes a broken sewing thread in one of Kafka's notebooks as a 'precious relic' and, though she concedes that this may sound 'absurd', later on she talks again of 'relics', 'worship' and 'hallowed objects'.

Andrew Motion glossed Larkin's theory of value by speaking of a 'primitive, visceral thrill' one feels when confronted with a manuscript produced by a famous author. But Larkin – and McLees – did not stop there. Another kind of value is involved here too: the 'meaningful value', which is 'of much more recent origin, and is the degree to which a manuscript helps to enlarge our knowledge and understanding of a writer's life and work', writes Larkin. 'A manuscript can show the cancellations, the substitutions, the shifting towards the ultimate form and the final meaning. A notebook, simply by being a fixed sequence of pages, can supply evidence of chronology. Unpublished work, unfinished work, even notes towards unwritten work all contribute to our knowledge of a writer's intentions; his letters and diaries add to what we know of his life and the circumstances in which he wrote.' Kafka is a case in point, as Malcolm Pasley, the lead editor of the first critical edition of his writings based on an extensive study of the manuscripts, memorably demonstrated.

Kafka's Manuscripts

Kafka's most famous novel, *The Trial*, tells the cryptic story of Josef K., a man arrested and prosecuted by an enigmatic court for a crime whose nature is never made clear to the reader – or, it would seem, even to Josef K. himself. For Umberto Eco, *The Trial* was a paradigmatic example of an 'open' work of literature – one that needs to be constructed by its readers as much as by its author. Malcolm Pasley is an extreme case of such an active reader, a reader who through his editorial work would go on to influence countless future readers. In 'Kafka's *Der Process*: What the Manuscript Can Tell Us', a lecture delivered in Oxford in 1990, he recounted his intimate study of the manuscript of *The Trial* in the late 1980s, when it was still kept in 'the ill-lit bowels of a Zurich bank', where he had to work 'under the eye of its owner' – Esther Hoffe, a woman who had found herself in the possession of Kafka's papers as a result of a process nearly as arcane as *Der Process* itself. Unlike in English, the German word that is the title of the novel means both 'trial' and 'process'. It is one of the great revelations that undergraduates have when they study the novel in the original: it opens up a whole host of new interpretative paths, suggesting as it does that this is not just a tale of a trial, but also of the process of writing itself, of telling tales.

Pasley did much to flesh out this idea. By examining the individual pages of the manuscript up close, not unlike an investigator hired by an unknown court, he was able to reconstruct an astonishing amount of information about Kafka's notoriously complicated writing process. Kafka had never finished work on *The Trial*, let alone published the novel; all he left behind were 'some 160 loose leaves' (Pasley counted them) that had not been arranged into a fixed order. Some of them formed longer, coherent chapters; some were just the opening lines of unfinished longer sections. Would editors of Kafka's work – or even individual readers – have to decide themselves what order to put them in? In the 1990s, a small German-Swiss publishing house produced an unconventional edition of the novel: sixteen chapters in loose bundles placed in a slipcase, to be arranged and rearranged by the reader herself.

But what interested Pasley was the fact that Kafka had originally written *The Trial* in a series of notebooks, and only later took them apart. 'Why did he do this? Puzzle No. 1', writes Pasley. Poring over the loose sheets, he noticed that almost all of them had been watermarked, and – more importantly – that 'the position of the watermark pattern had varied from quire to quire and from book to book'. This discovery, and a series of cross-comparisons with other manuscripts kept at Oxford, allowed Pasley to ascertain that various sections of *The Trial* had been written down in notebooks containing other drafts. Kafka needed to take them apart so he could gather all the bits of his novel in one place. Puzzle No. 1 – solved.

But then there was Puzzle No. 2: in what order did Kafka write the different sections of *The Trial*, scattered across those various notebooks? To answer this question, Pasley decided to examine another feature of the manuscript absent from printed editions: the size of Kafka's handwriting, which 'underwent a most remarkable change during the five months or so when he was engaged on *Der Process*'. More counting was required.

Pasley established that in the two years before Kafka

started work on *The Trial*, he would write about 200 words on average on each page of his standard-sized notebooks. But in the seven years after he abandoned the draft, he would write some 350 words on a page of the same size. A comparison with other, more easily datable drafts from the decade in question confirmed that 'the contraction of the script had proceeded progressively in a linear fashion'. After a 'rather painful excursion into mathematics', as he put it, Pasley concluded that Kafka wrote most of the manuscript in the first two months of work on the draft – and then got stuck.

'It was evidently not just Josef K.'s *Process* that was going badly: Franz Kafka's "*Process*"' – his writing process – 'had run into serious trouble as well', says Pasley. But Kafka, used to tormenting himself over unfinished drafts, seems to have anticipated such a turn of events. He decided to start by writing the opening *and* closing sequences of the novel – Josef K.'s arrest and death – first. This was the most significant discovery that Pasley made: by analysing the watermarked paper and the number of words per page, he was able to prove that those two passages were written one straight after the other.

And so, Pasley writes, 'the *process* in which Josef K. is involved, and the process of its invention and inscription, seem to hang mysteriously together'. He goes on to quote from the closing passage of the novel, where Josef K. asks himself: 'Shall they say of me that at the beginning of my trial I wanted to end it, and now, at its end, I want to begin it again?' But in the original German, as Pasley's meticulous research demonstrated, this sentence describes Kafka's writing process too. He wrote the ending of the novel when he was just beginning to work on it – and once the ending had been committed to paper, it was time to go back to the beginning of the plot. Such are the delightful discoveries that manuscripts can yield: a perfect example of their meaningful value.

Precious Like Papyrus

In the webinar on Kafka's manuscripts, Fiona McLees goes on to add a third kind of value to Larkin's scheme: material value. This one might be hard to swallow for readers who like to think of Kafka's works as pure, transcendent art, the value of which cannot be measured in money. But the fact is that his manuscripts – even postcards or handwritten short notes – bring in huge sums at auctions. In 1988 the German Literature Archive in Marbach reportedly paid nearly $2 million for the manuscript of *The Trial*, a sum identified by *The New York Times* as 'the highest price ever paid for a modern manuscript' at the time. A mercantile metaphor slips into McLees's talk: she repeatedly speaks of 'stakeholders' when talking about the people who are invested in the manuscripts, even as she apologises for the term each time.

But perhaps this is to be expected: we regularly talk of value in these terms – I just talked of people *invested* in the manuscripts myself – and so did Kafka. For example, the German word for guilt – 'Schuld' – also means debt, including in the literal, monetary sense. In *The Metamorphosis*, Gregor Samsa thinks with trepidation of his father's 'Schuld' which he tries to help pay off by working overtime; the immediate context suggests that a monetary debt is at stake but, in the context of the story as a whole, it is fair to say that a sense of ill-defined, metaphysical guilt affects Gregor and his fraught relationship with his family, too.

At the same time, Kafka did not treat his manuscripts as objects of material value, but rather as working drafts, as McLees makes clear. She likes the way Kafka's biographer Reiner Stach put it: 'No author at the beginning of the twentieth century – least of all Kafka himself – could have imagined that his written legacy would soon be measured, photographed, and described as though it were a set of papyrus rolls from an Egyptian burial chamber.' In fact, he did not seem to think they should survive at all.

Kafka famously asked his closest friend, Max Brod, to burn his manuscripts after his death, but Brod disregarded that request and posthumously published Kafka's writings. But the truth might be more complicated than that. Kafka knew that Brod was his greatest champion, always enthusiastic about his writing, always trying to persuade him to publish more, arranging for publication of this or that story here and there, holding on to every scrap of writing that Kafka would give him. And this was despite Brod being a writer himself, in fact, much better known and more successful than Kafka at the time, underscoring his selfless dedication to Kafka's legacy. After Kafka's death, Brod claimed that Kafka must have realised that he could never bring himself to burn the manuscripts: in asking him of all people to carry out his supposed wish, Kafka in fact ensured their survival. Brod eventually went down in history primarily as Kafka's most important reader, rather than a writer in his own right.

He held on to his friend's manuscripts even as he was hurriedly leaving Prague for Palestine on the last train before the Nazis closed the Czech border in 1939. The next eighty years would see various wads of these precious papers move back and forth between Israel, Germany, Switzerland – and England. The history of the manuscripts 'could be the subject of a full-length adventure novel or movie', writes Germanist Osman Durrani. As I listen to McLees, I think about the curious chapter of that history which brought the most substantial portion of the manuscripts to Oxford.

In 1960, a young British aristocrat, born in India during the British Raj, now a fellow in German at Magdalen College, found out from one of his undergraduates that Kafka's grandnephew was studying law at another Oxford college. The Germanist in question was none other than Malcolm Pasley, soon to be the world's most famous scholar and editor of Kafka's manuscripts. More discoveries followed: the student's mother, Marianne Steiner, lived in London, and she and Kafka's few other surviving relatives were the legal owners of most of Kafka's manuscripts, even though it was Brod who had held them in his possession for many years. In fact, he had moved most of them to a Swiss bank vault a few years earlier, fearing for their safety in Israel during the Suez Crisis. Kafka's heirs now agreed to Pasley's suggestion that the manuscripts be moved from Zurich to Oxford and deposited in the Bodleian Library. More papers soon followed from other sources. Since then, some have passed into the library's possession, and others are owned jointly by the Bodleian and the children of one of Kafka's sisters.

In 1961, the core manuscripts arrived. But how exactly? As Pasley would soon write in the first article that listed all of these papers for other interested scholars to see, 'the somewhat unexpected arrival in this country of these remarkable documents' was preceded by 'a series of not inappropriate vicissitudes and wanderings'. He did not specify his own role in these, which did not stop at talking to Kafka's heirs. Pasley brought the manuscripts to Oxford himself, in his own car. As Jim Reed, one of his colleagues at Oxford, would later reminisce, 'his journey has become a legend among scholars of German'.

While on a skiing trip in the Alps, Pasley got word that the last bureaucratic obstacles had been cleared and the manuscripts were ready for collection in Zurich. He packed up his skis, bought an extra suitcase, walked into the bank ('the wintry arrival and the confrontation with officials had atmospheric echoes of Kafka's *Castle* and *Trial*', Reed commented), took out insurance at a travel agency down the street, got into his small Fiat (given that one of the manuscripts he was to transport was *The Metamorphosis* it seems a missed opportunity that it was not a Volkswagen Beetle, as Reed pointed out), and drove off.

Kevin Hilliard, another of Pasley's Oxford colleagues, wondered at how 'this model gentleman understood the mind of one of the most idiosyncratic and radical writers of the twentieth century better than anyone else in his time'. The same question hangs over an article about Pasley titled 'Kafka's Half-Brother', written by a reporter from the German weekly *Die Zeit* who visited Pasley in his north Oxford home in 1992. By then, Pasley had become a fellow of the British Academy and inherited his father's baronetcy. That is the mystery of cultural affinity: through reading, we can imaginatively inhabit worlds very different from our own. By tracing the history of extraordinary investments

– both actual and metaphoric – in Kafka's manuscripts that his readers have made over the last century across borders of language, nationality, history and class, we can begin to appreciate just how inadequate traditional literary histories are when they refuse to follow texts as they cross these lines.

We can also start to see more clearly that the meaning of books can often be found in the reasons why readers find them personally significant. I matriculated at Magdalen College exactly half a century after the manuscripts' arrival in Oxford, although I did not realise it at the time. I never met Pasley: he retired from teaching in 1986 and died in 2004, after years of suffering from multiple sclerosis. Yet I feel his presence, editorial at least, every time I flick open my edition of *The Trial* or *The Metamorphosis*; Pasley led the editorial team that produced the standard critical edition of Kafka's works. But while I have much admiration for these two classics, I have always felt especially drawn to Kafka's least-known novel, *The Man who Disappeared*, the enigmatic story of Karl, a teenage immigrant from Eastern Europe who travels to America on his own, where he has to find his way around this new country. In Kafka's world, there is space for all sorts of different characters – and readers.

Pandemic Read

As the coronavirus pandemic rages around the world, one text in particular seems to come into its own: *Die Verwandlung* or, as it is known in the English-speaking world, *The Metamorphosis*. Perhaps it is purely because the story of Gregor Samsa, a travelling salesman who 'woke one morning from troubled dreams' only to find himself 'transformed right there in his bed into some sort of monstrous insect', written in 1912 and published in 1915, is Kafka's most widely read tale. But I think there is more to it: the violent metaphor of an ostensibly ordinary person changing into a disgusting bug who now has to be confined to his own room seems to resonate with both the pandemic and Brexit, the other crisis engulfing Britain at the time, though in different ways.

Here is how I would have recounted the plot of *The Metamorphosis* before 2020. One day, Gregor Samsa wakes up in the body of an 'ungeheures Ungeziefer'. The term 'Ungeziefer' initially designated animals regarded as 'unclean' and therefore unsuitable for religious sacrifice, and later bugs or rodents; it was also used as an insult. 'Ungeheuer' features the same negative prefix and means 'gigantic' or, in medieval German, 'uncanny'. It is difficult to picture what such 'monstrous vermin' might look like exactly, although the description makes it clear that it is some kind of insect – but the curious lack of specificity of the phrase 'ungeheures Ungeziefer' might encourage readers to treat this creature as a symbol or metaphor instead. Gregor himself does not spend much time contemplating his strange transformation, and neither does his family, even though they are shocked by it. They all focus on practical challenges posed by Gregor's transformation. Can he move? (First with difficulty, then more comfortably as he learns to control his new body.) Can he talk? (Not really: his voice is unrecognisable, so he soon stops trying to communicate in this way.) Can he go to work? (Despite his initial hope that he might still be able to catch a morning train, he gives up after a disastrous visit from the chief clerk at his office.) What can he eat? (Fresh food does not taste so good, but he does enjoy all kinds of half-rotten leftovers.) How to bear looking at him? (Gregor starts hiding under the couch when others enter his room to spare them this dilemma.) How best to set up his room now that he is a monstrous insect? (Here Gregor's wishes go against his sister Grete's designs. When she attempts to remove all his furniture and belongings, apparently to provide more crawling space for him, Gregor is distraught.)

While Grete, at least initially, takes care of her brother, his feeble, sickly mother mostly keeps away, and his elderly, weakly father thrusts his walking stick at him to force him back into his room. But slowly the family undergoes a transformation too. For one thing, the father takes up a job, even though for years Gregor has believed him to be infirm and so worked hard to support the entire family. He also seems to become stronger: after the incident with the walking stick, another time that Gregor emerges from his room, Mr Samsa throws apples at him, one of which seriously injures Gregor. Grete, too, becomes more independent and starts to neglect Gregor. One night, she plays the violin – a pursuit that Gregor has always supported – to the three grotesque lodgers whom the family has taken in. When Gregor crawls out of his room to get closer to Grete and her music, the lodgers notice him and leave the apartment in outrage. That is when Grete decides that they have all had enough: the family must get rid of him – or rather, it. (In the manuscript, Kafka crossed out the masculine pronoun and replaced it with the inhuman 'it'.) Gregor feels ashamed and dies in the small hours, leaving his family relieved and happy, full of hope for the future.

But when I reread the story in 2020, all sorts of new

details catch my attention. Gregor Samsa wakes up locked in his room – 'a little on the small side' – in a house opposite a hospital, with a collection of textiles on the table, which he is used to peddling every day as a travelling salesman: 'On the road, day in, day out.' But now something has happened to his body overnight; something is wrong. Gregor considers 'calling in sick'. Is he sick, though? He does not think so. But then his voice sounds strange because there is some strange 'squeaking' in it, as though coming 'from below'; it must be the beginning of 'a head cold'– easy to catch when one travels around and meets 'new people all the time'. He coughs to try and clear his throat. He struggles to raise his body and get out of bed, so he lies still a little longer, 'his breathing shallow'.

Gregor knows that he is likely to lose his job as a result of all this – even though 'what he was now experiencing' could also 'befall the general manager'. But the company for which Samsa works is strict: 'a season for doing no business at all, Herr Samsa, there is no such thing, and there cannot be', he is told. Gregor worries that losing his job would put the livelihood of his entire family at risk. His parents are vulnerable: his father is elderly and obese, and his mother has asthma and often has difficulty breathing. Trying to persuade the manager to let him keep his job, Gregor tries to go back to the idea that he is sick – yes, has been feeling sickly for a couple of days now: 'But we always just assume we'll be able to overcome these illnesses without staying home.' Yet his voice is so deformed as to be unintelligible, so Gregor's family calls for a doctor; he must be very sick indeed; nobody dares enter his room; in the Samsa household, 'a great misfortune has taken place'.

Gregor's life is entirely disrupted; he is treated like a 'gravely ill patient' and his room gets scrupulously locked up, so that his only glimpse of the outer world is through the windows. Soon he is literally crawling up the walls. When his sister Grete comes in to clean the room twice a day, she first runs to open the windows to ventilate the space. Gregor's parents do not visit him in his room for two weeks – Gregor is worried that seeing him might make his mother sick, even cause her to die; her breathing difficulties increase: at one point she begins to 'cough dully into her lifted hand' – but the family still hopes to see 'some sign of an improvement in Gregor's condition' soon.

Two months pass, though, and he is actually deteriorating further. He also feels like 'the absence of all direct human address, combined with the monotony of life in his family's midst' is starting to get to him. Physical exertion is dangerous now: 'a shortness of breath began to set in – even in his earlier life his lungs had been none too reliable'; to move across his room, he now needs 'many, many minutes' – 'like an old invalid'. Now Gregor's sister also thinks he's a threat to his parents' health: 'It'll be the death of you two, I can see it now', she says. At this point, Gregor's body is in pain. Soon 'his final breath passe[s] feebly from his nostrils'. Gregor dies and his family leaves the house together for the first time in many months.

Of course, there is a good explanation for all this. Gregor is now a huge insect: that is why he finds it difficult to move his body around, that is why he is feeling odd, almost sick, why his voice sounds strange; he breathes heavily because he has been trying to lug around his new heavy body, not because he contracted coronavirus on his travels and passed it on to his mother. His textile collection consists of fabrics that he sells rather than face masks, and at the beginning of the story he is locked up in his room because he always locks it overnight and now struggles to open the door, and does not want his family and boss to see him in his new insect body anyway – he was not put under lockdown, placed into quarantine. And he is feeling isolated and distanced from others because of his transformation into an insect and increasingly fraught power relations in the family, not because of government-mandated self-isolation and social distancing.

And yet there is something about Gregor's situation that resonates with readers in the age of coronavirus, and not entirely by chance. The most striking feature of Kafka's tale is how Gregor is presented with a new, shocking reality – he now lives in an insect's body – but he, and soon everybody around him too, adapts to it without much questioning at all, concentrating on purely practical aspects of his new situation. Gregor focuses almost all of his attention on questions like: which new limbs to use to climb out of bed? how best to handle his boss's ire? which train might he still be able to catch? It is only the briefest of moments that Samsa spends motionless, 'in the expectation, perhaps, that this perfect silence might possibly restore the real and ordinary state of things'.

Kafka and Coronavirus

By paying attention to how Kafka is being read in the age of coronavirus, we can learn something both about his writings and about our own experience of the pandemic. Seen through the lens of Kafka's works, the pandemic emerges as a realization of a deep-seated fear, a nightmarish scenario that we have been working through in our modernist classics: the fear of entrapment in one's own home, of losing control of one's own body, an unforeseen and violent disruption of daily life. Seen through the lens of the pandemic, Kafka's preoccupation with ill health, raspy breathing and lung infections comes to the fore. His characters, we realise, are not abstract ciphers, embodied allegories – rather, they are living, breathing things, held captive by the fragility of their own bodies.

In February 2020, the premiere of a theatrical adaptation of *The Metamorphosis* by a Scottish company, Vanishing Point, is cancelled: the pandemic has hit northern Italy, where the production was supposed to be staged at a festival. It premieres in mid-March in Glasgow instead, mere days before the first national lockdown is announced in the UK. 'It's hard not to see a metaphor for the pandemic' in Matthew Lenton's production, writes a reviewer for the *Guardian*; the actor playing Gregor transformed into an insect ends up 'fumigated by figures in protective clothing'. Another reviewer describes how the adaptation 'brings home the everyday hysteria that exists in a Brexit-scarred, Covid-19 consumed landscape'; a third calls it a 'horrifyingly timely adaptation'. From the early days of the pandemic, *The Metamorphosis* becomes one of the key cultural scripts to try to grasp Covid-19's impact on our collective psyche.

Once the country is put under lockdown in the spring of 2020, undergraduates at the University of Sheffield read *The Metamorphosis* and watch the Royal Ballet's 2011 adaptation. One of the students is struck by 'the lack of control' that Gregor Samsa 'feels over his body', which 'resonates with the lack of control over [her] own body that [she has] been feeling during lockdown'; 'many people are currently at odds with their bodies', she adds. Arthur Pita, the choreographer of the ballet, begins hearing from others who watch it while in quarantine and find it 'cathartic'. While we remain physically distanced from each other and yet hyperaware of our bodies, Gregor Samsa offers a compelling point of identification for many. By the beginning of the summer, German theatre group Lokstoff! takes to a large car park in Stuttgart to perform a socially distanced adaptation of *The Metamorphosis* titled *BEFORE/AFTER: The Metamorphosis of the World*. Each actor is enclosed in an individual Zorb ball – during the performance, extra oxygen has to be pumped into the balls – while the spectators stay in their cars. A local radio station reports that the whole play feels as though performed in a 'maximum security unit': a suitable metaphor for the estrangement of the coronavirus pandemic.

By the end of the summer, Hijinx, a Welsh theatre company that works with actors who have learning disabilities and autism, produces a live play on Zoom, an adaptation of *The Metamorphosis*, channelling 'some of the feelings of loneliness and fears for the future, isolation, and a sense of loss of worth', according to the artistic director Ben Pettitt-Wade. A BBC journalist; an Indian economist; a Greek sociologist; people from many walks of life find solace in Kafka's eerie tale of a man turned into a bug, locked up in a small room for weeks on end. One headline in an online literary magazine reads 'We Are All Gregor Samsa Now'. A professor of creative writing in Arkansas asks his students to write 'plague diaries' as they shelter in place. He is thinking of Kafka's incessant diary writing: 'I wanted a mountain of words to act as a shield against the unknowable', he explains. Two Irish doctors report in the journal *Medical Humanities* that they are immersing themselves in Kafka's works during lockdown. Life feels 'oppressive and nightmarish'; 'feelings of estrangement and helplessness' come to the fore; Kafka's texts seem well suited to work through these emotions, perhaps not least because of the central image of a bug: as a researcher at Harvard Medical School will show in her analysis of 6,000 dreams reported during the coronavirus pandemic, a significant number involved 'dozens and dozens and dozens of every kind of bug imaginable attacking the dreamer'.

Kafka himself would go on to understand respiratory illness in all its terrifying, intimate detail. Following a series of haemorrhages in 1917, five years after writing *The Metamorphosis*, he was diagnosed with tuberculosis. For years before his diagnosis, Kafka had already complained of weakness and frailty; from as early as 1905, he repeatedly stayed in spa towns and sanatoria. 'For a long time I've been complaining that I am always ill but never have a particular illness that would force me to lie down in bed', he wrote, tongue-in-cheek, in his diary in 1911. Soon this would change. In 1918, when Europe was being ravaged by the Spanish flu epidemic, he contracted that disease too: he developed a fever of 40°C and ended up with a bad case of pneumonia. And yet Kafka would still often adopt a humorous, playful tone when commenting on his health, at least outwardly. In a letter to Oskar Baum, one of his closest friends, sometimes dated to 1918 and sometimes to 1920, Kafka wrote:

In medical terms this is simply a hopeless case, in jest and in earnest. Would you care for a lay diagnosis? The physical illness is just an overflow of the spiritual illness. If one tries to stem its flow, then the head naturally defends itself, since in a time of need it has spawned the lung disease and now one is trying to force it back up there, just when the head feels the strongest need to spawn still other diseases. Moreover to begin with the head and cure it would require the strength of a furniture mover, which for the aforementioned reason I will never be able to summon up.

Both in 1918 and 1920, Kafka took extended leave from work and travelled to the countryside and various health resorts in an attempt to improve his symptoms – but all in vain. As his health deteriorated, he spent more and more time on sick leave, finally leading to an early retirement from his job as a high-ranking lawyer in a large insurance agency in 1923. A year later, at the age of forty, Kafka's condition worsened again: the tuberculosis spread to his throat; he struggled to take in any food at all. He died in the summer of 1924.

Kafka and Brexit

As Kafka lay stricken with influenza in the autumn of 1918, something else was afoot too. The First World War was over, bringing with it the dissolution of the Austro-Hungarian Empire. Kafka 'contract[ed] a fever as a subject in the Habsburg Monarchy and reemerg[ed] from it as a citizen of a Czech democracy', writes Reiner Stach; 'the flu and politics went hand in hand'. A century later, Britain reached the peak of the coronavirus pandemic just after it left the European Union.

As readers, we regularly see a reflection of our own times, our own crises, in the books we particularly value, especially those that seem pregnant with nebulous metaphorical meaning. Literature feels universal not when it does not seem anchored to any specific place or time, but when readers find themselves anchoring it to their own time and place, over and over again. And so it was not just the coronavirus pandemic that Kafka's *Metamorphosis* seemed to resonate with in 2020. Brexit prompted similar comparisons too.

In at least one case, the comparison went mainstream. In the autumn of 2019, Ian McEwan published a novella called *The Cockroach*. The opening pages were published in the *Guardian*; the accompanying audiobook was narrated by the actor Bill Nighy. As I said: a mainstream event, at least in comparison to the baseline level of buzz that usually surrounds modernist German literature in Britain. It is easy to lose sight of just how meaningful an event this was: one of the most successful contemporary British writers reacts to one of the most significant political events of his life by writing his own version of one of the most famous short stories ever written in Europe. If we want to understand why Kafka still matters today, then surely this is one of the best case studies we have at our disposal.

Here is how *The Cockroach* begins: 'That morning, Jim Sams, clever but by no means profound, woke from uneasy dreams to find himself transformed into a gigantic creature.' Where Kafka's Samsa marvelled at his many small insect legs, McEwan's Sams 'regarded his distant feet, his paucity of limbs, with consternation'. McEwan's elegant satiric style comes into its own when describing Sams's newly human tongue: 'An organ, a slab of slippery meat, lay squat and wet in his mouth – revolting, especially when it moved of its own accord to explore the vast cavern of his mouth and, he noted with muted alarm, slide across an immensity of teeth.' He luxuriates in the descriptions of the more disgusting aspects of being human, channelling his protagonist's predilections as a cockroach at heart: 'The light breeze that blew inter-mittently across [his chest], bearing a not unattractive odour of decomposing food and grain alcohol, he accepted as his breath.'

As he observes a small insect cautiously crawl out of his bedroom – 'no doubt the displaced owner of the body he now inhabited' – Sams begins to realise that said body is that of the prime minister of the United Kingdom. But his true nature as a cockroach is still made clear at every turn: that first morning, for example, he cannot focus on shop talk because a dying bluebottle makes him think about how delicious it would be ('a cheese flavour. Stilton, mostly'). To put it bluntly, everything that is said about PM Jim Sams potentially applies to the real-life British PM in 2019.

Where lies the boundary between thought-provoking satire and unproductive offensiveness, as tasteless as it is elitist? Jim Sams behaves like a disgusting insect, fantasises about eating dung, can barely speak, does not understand much, 'his immediate concern [is] to appear plausible' – which makes sense, since he is barely even human at all. When chairing a Cabinet meeting, Sams realises that almost all its members are insects, instantly recognisable 'through their transparent, superficial human form'. They now form the 'metamorphosed' Cabinet – a nod to the title of Kafka's story. They are 'inspired by an idea as pure and thrilling as blood and soil', which might refer to the literal blood and literal soil that bugs are drawn to, but also inevitably makes us think of the Nazi 'Blut und Boden' ideology.

In the second part of the story, we learn more about the bizarre ideological movement that McEwan has concocted as a transparent metaphor for Brexit: the so-called Reversalism. Long considered 'a thought experiment, an after-dinner game, a joke', through a series of political mishaps and blunders Reversalism becomes the official agenda of the government. The goal is to reverse the flow of money in the United Kingdom: employees have to pay their employers rather than the other way round, and they have to shop to be able to afford it – since it is now shop-owners who pay their customers. Those who oppose Reversalism are snubbed, and dubbed 'Clockwisers'. Archie Tupper, a thinly veiled Donald Trump spoof, swiftly gets on board and tweets out in support of the British PM in his usual style – 'it was poetry, smoothly combining density of meaning with fleet-footed liberation from detail'.

Jim Sams, cockroach-turned-PM, works hard to discredit the 'Clockwisers' in his own party who attempt to stop his reforms. In one particularly unsavoury episode, he pens a fabricated piece on sexual harassment, to be submitted to the *Guardian* under the name of a female colleague with the goal of sinking the career of a troublesome Cabinet member. He finds that 'There was nothing more liberating than a closely knit sequence of lies. So this was why people became writers.' Any conceivable standards of public service are in tatters; the only goal is to manically press forward with Reversalism, which the government does manage to legislate. And then it all ends: the politicians turn back into bugs. They did it all because – everything is carefully spelt out for us in this transparent moral – they thrive on death, poverty and squalor. That is why they were so committed to the government's reckless revolution.

McEwan described *The Cockroach* as 'political satire in an old tradition'. 'Mockery might be a therapeutic response, though it's hardly a solution', he added. Others have given it a decidedly more contemporary label: 'Brexlit', largely penned by middle-class 'Remoaners' who have nothing but scorn and contempt for anybody who does not share their views. How therapeutic can this 'Brexlit' really be? Unsurprisingly, reviews in a certain segment of the press were sceptical, to say the least. In the *Evening Standard*, David Sexton called *The Cockroach* 'patronising', and a 'self-satisfied amusement'. But others were cautious, too. 'Comparing one's political opponents to cockroaches is a toxic metaphor with a nasty political history and it is hard to read McEwan's novella without a degree of discomfort', wrote Fintan O'Toole in the *Guardian*, even though he still called the novella a 'comic triumph'. One German reviewer was similarly discomfited by the brutality of McEwan's language, the talk of excrement and disgust; she felt that it was an inappropriate artistic response to the failure of the British elites. This sense was shared by Christopher John Stephens in *Pop Matters*: 'The metaphor of a politician as a parasite on humanity is as subtle as a hammer.' He added: 'In these times, readers deserve much better.'

What do we learn about Kafka – and Brexit – by looking closely at *The Cockroach* and the discussion it generated?

It is a particularly tangible example of how Kafka has furnished later writers with lasting images of abjection and visceral contempt in a world of senseless bureaucracy and political crisis. But it also stages a ruthless confrontation with the failure of British culture to generate a positive alternative to the Brexit narrative. The resounding success of Kafka's *Metamorphosis* throws into sharp relief the ultimate failure of McEwan's *Cockroach* – and vice versa. A couple of years before the publication of *The Cockroach*, a mock-up of a distinctive orange Penguin cover made the rounds on Twitter: *Brexit*, a novel by Franz Kafka. Half joke, half fantasy: as Leo Robson wrote of McEwan's project in the *New Statesman*, the hope is that 'one of the 20th century's great writers' can help us 'comprehend one of the great political crises of the 21st'. But *The Cockroach* did not quite live up to the task.

And yet the peculiar stickiness of Kafka and his literary world stubbornly persists in discussions of the British political scene, across the ideological spectrum. In the summer of 2022, the *Daily Mail* ran an article about Boris Johnson's investigation by the Commons Committee of Privileges, titled 'A Kafkaesque Kangaroo Court', apparently citing Johnson's allies. The paper's editors must have worried, though, that its readers might not be familiar with the term, so they provided a definition in a little box at the bottom of the page, alongside a photograph of Kafka: fair enough. Except that it is a highly idiosyncratic definition, which becomes obvious as soon as one takes in its oversized heading: 'Word that's totally alien to Britain's values of freedom.' 'In his book, *The Trial*, Kafka described a man pursued by shadowy authorities for a crime which they would not even name as he is driven to the depths of misery', we learn. The possibility of Josef K.'s guilt, indeed of his perverse desire to get punished, is not entertained. The peculiar definition continues instead: 'For centuries, the British have lived in a free country where such things were unknown. Now the Prime Minister's friends fear such a calumny is happening to our most high-profile politician.'

While McEwan used Kafka's work as a lens through which to criticise Johnson's government and its commitment to 'getting Brexit done', Johnson's supporters drew on it to criticise his critics, and the *Daily Mail* attempted to frame it as an expression of European bureaucratic structures, allegedly antithetical to the British political culture – precisely the kind of structures, one is left to assume, that Brexit was supposed to deliver us from. It is safe to say that few other dead writers, British or otherwise, have been instrumentalised so much in public discussions about Brexit, and it is important for us scholars to acknowledge the uncommon, quite frankly astounding, power of Kafka's spectral presence in the public imagination, while also correcting the misconceptions that have emerged in the process. Some of these misconceptions have to do with the interpretation of Kafka's works, but others are more basic: in the *Daily Mail*, Kafka is introduced as a 'Czech' writer. In the next chapter, we will tackle both the question of what a text like *The Metamorphosis* really means – and how we might know this – and how such meaning might be connected to Kafka's identity, including the loaded question of his nationality.

2

Berlin

German Kafka

Siegfried Doesn't Get It

I would like to introduce you to two readers of Kafka who will not only provide a useful bridge from twenty-first-century Oxford to early twentieth-century Germany, but also give us a chance to revisit *The Metamorphosis*, the story we encountered in the last chapter, to interrogate again the question that all self-respecting readers want to have answered: what it really *means*.

Enter one Siegfried Wolff of Berlin, a highly educated banker and war veteran. He is the author of the only surviving letter Kafka ever received from a reader outside of his friendship group, in 1917 – but it was not exactly fan mail. 'Dear Sir, You have made me unhappy', the letter opens. 'I bought your *Metamorphosis* and gave it to my cousin. But she doesn't know how to make sense of the story.' Other family members are also at a loss. Worse still, Wolff himself does not know what to make of it, despite his reputation as the wise man of the family. 'So please tell me', he writes to Kafka, 'what my cousin is supposed to think when she reads *The Metamorphosis*.'

When I first read this letter, I thought it must be a fake: it seemed too good to be true! It is such a funny and quaint vignette of the irreducibility of Kafka's writing, and the discomfort it generates in readers. But in fact it does seem to be authentic, even though a reply from Kafka has not been preserved. Or maybe he never wrote one: after all, as I will try to persuade you in this chapter, withholding an answer to Wolff's insistent questioning might have been the most fitting response by an author who is so attractively difficult to pin down.

How much can we learn from Wolff's amusing missive? Not much, you might think – but one of the most exciting parts of the job of a literary historian is to be able to make documents such as these speak to us. First of all, Wolff's letter shows that, although one might expect a contemporary reader to have more insight into the cultural context that surrounded Kafka's work, the meaning of *The Metamorphosis* was far from obvious during his lifetime. Understanding what it was like to live in Central Europe during the first decades of the twentieth century will certainly deepen our understanding of Kafka, but it will not explain away the wonderful strangeness of his work. Even understanding the place of Jewish people in this narrative will not give us all the answers. As it happens, Siegfried Wolff was Jewish too – but he did not seem to recognise in *The Metamorphosis* an allegory for his experience as a Jewish man, although (as we will see in Chapter Four) that is a reading of the text which is frequently advanced.

We might also want to rethink hasty claims about Kafka's story as a straightforward metaphor for the suffering and confusion of wartime – an assumption sometimes made by readers, and certainly many of my students. 'Sir! I spent months in the trenches slugging it out with the Russians and didn't bat an eyelash', writes Wolff to Kafka; 'But if my reputation with my cousins went to the devil, I couldn't bear it.' For this reader, the experience of reading Kafka's story does seem to bear some obscure relationship to his experience of the war, but its exact nature is not immediately clear.

People often say about Kafka that he captured the shock and disorientation wrought by the sudden onslaught of modernity, from the first major experience of mechanical warfare to irreversible changes in traditional family structure. If you want to understand – if you want to viscerally feel – what this might have really meant to Kafka's readers in the 1910s, just read Wolff's letter really closely. *The Metamorphosis* is an irritant: confronted with the enigma of Kafka's story, a respectable bourgeois man loses his bearings; his inability to see through it really pushes him to the brink. He draws a link between his experience of the war and his inability to comprehend *The Metamorphosis*, which threatens his position of authority within the family – much like how Gregor's position of power in the story is challenged because of his transformation.

But panicked uncertainty in the face of Kafka's writing is not unique to his contemporaries, as becomes clear when we read Wolff's letter alongside another document – though one much more recent, and much closer to home.

Somebody Else Doesn't Get It Either

In the summer of 2021, Kafka had his moment on Twitter.

41

It turned out that Richard Dawkins, the eminent British evolutionary biologist, does not appreciate the possible metaphorical resonances of a story about a man who turns – dare I say evolves? – into an insect overnight.

'Kafka's *Metamorphosis* is called a major work of literature. Why? If it's SF it's bad SF. If, like *Animal Farm*, it's an allegory, an allegory of what? Scholarly answers range from pretentious Freudian to far-fetched feminist. I don't get it. Where are the Emperor's clothes?' Dawkins tweeted.

Hundreds of responses promptly poured in – including one from Philip Pullman. 'Richard, you once coined the excellent phrase "the argument from personal incredulity": I can't believe this, so it's not true. Aren't you providing an example of that very thing? "I don't get it, so everyone else is wrong".' As it happens, Dawkins is a fellow of one of Oxford's colleges, and Pullman a graduate of another; his famous fantasy trilogy *His Dark Materials* is set here. But even if this discussion of Kafka started out as a local affair, it quickly went global.

You might think that no respectable scholar of literature should waste their time on a Twitterstorm like this. But I disagree: Dawkins's tweet seems to bear more than a passing resemblance to Wolff's letter of 1917, and the novelty of our communication technologies today should not distract us from the fact that, however imperfectly, they allow us to take the pulse of diverse reading habits and experiences in the way that letters, diaries and marginal notes did before the rise of the Internet. What both Wolff's letter and Dawkins's tweet make clear is that the traditional repertoire of responses to literary texts falls short when it comes to Kafka, and this can be disorientating as it frustrates readers' desire to easily get something out of the text, to extract meaning without too much fuss.

But the feelings of disorientation and frustration are in fact a key part of the meaning of Kafka's enigmatic story, not least because they mirror the emotions Gregor Samsa's experience stirs up in him and his family. Many readers recognise this: sifting past some inevitably unhelpful tweets – offensive, mocking, widely off topic – I was struck by how many of the responses to Dawkins's provocative question were actually very helpful. And the vast, vast majority defended Kafka – and, by extension, literature – rather than siding with Dawkins.

Many readers decided to use their precious 280 characters to offer plausible micro-interpretations of Kafka's story, often implicitly or explicitly connected to their lived experience, in some cases even managing to squeeze in telling details from the story (like the behaviour of the Samsa family after Gregor's death) or Kafka's life (like his work in the field of accident insurance). For example, one popular response, from a user who described themselves in their profile as a 'neurodivergent humanist', read: 'It's simply about alienation, isolation and inferiority in working class communities. It captures what happens when those around you stop regarding you as human.'

The characters in the story are not working class, and nor was Kafka – in class terms, the story is more about various threats to stable and secure middle-class life – but something about this interpretation nevertheless rings true. Many, many tweets suggested that the alienation that Gregor experiences is closely linked to the ills of the capitalist system. A professor of physics from Shanghai wrote: 'It's about how quickly your family and society would turn on you if you stopped being productive or indeed convenient', also earning lots of likes. An engineer from California added: 'As a breadwinner cancer survivor, I can totally relate to Gregor Samsa trying to tell his boss that, yes, he's coming to work, when he is a giant bug who has trouble getting out of bed.' A clinical health psychologist chimed in to say that the story is used in public health curricula to teach students about disease and stigma.

Other commentators on Twitter thought that *The Metamorphosis* does not belong to any of the genres Dawkins listed in his tweet and threw other aesthetic labels into the mix: 'surrealism,' 'existentialism,' 'tragedy,' 'satire,' 'absurdism,' 'magical realism'. Still others questioned this approach by challenging the assumption that identifying the genre of a text can explain away its meaning. Perhaps as a biologist used to the explanatory power of taxonomy, Dawkins puts too much faith in the explanatory power of genre labels.

Then there were those who tried to unpack the underlying assumptions about literary value in Dawkins's tweet further still, using terms like 'utilitarianism', 'elitism', 'ambiguity', 'complexity', 'canonisation', 'taste', 'objectivity' and 'subjectivity'. Some particularly canny commentators linked their interpretation of Kafka's story to those very assumptions: one writer (interested in political history and policy) quipped that the story shows what happens when people are only valued in terms of their usefulness – just like Dawkins might have implied that literature is only valuable when it has a clear use.

As it turns out, paying close attention to readers who find Kafka's writing resistant to interpretation is an extremely valuable exercise: it allows us to better understand the expectations that readers tend to bring to literary texts – for example, that their meaning should be obvious and unambiguous – and the mechanisms through which Kafka subverts these expectations – for example, by presenting us with stories that operate with tantalisingly precise, evocative images which taunt us by leaving their meaning open to interpretation. It is similarly worthwhile to listen to readers who describe how the books they cherish have affected their lives, however reluctant we might be to do so, perhaps trained to feel 'nervous about literature's awkward proximity to imagination, emotion, and other soft, fuzzy ideas', as literary scholar Rita Felski put it. But listening to readers' stories allows us to recognise the intellectual and emotional payoff that awaits those who stick with the discomfort a writer like Kafka generates in readers. This is not just literary theory: this is literature in practice, literature as it matters to us.

So You Want People to Know Kafka Wrote in German?

To contend with the disorientation triggered by Kafka's writing it is useful to pay close attention both to readers who find it off-putting, and those who embrace it. But there is another type of complexity to Kafka that we need to grasp in order to fully appreciate his literary universe – and here the more traditional tools of a literary historian will come in handy.

This idea was brought home to me in the conceptual meeting about Oxford's big Kafka exhibition in 2024. Picture a room with five academics trying to distil what it is that they want visitors, who in most cases will not know much about Kafka, to learn about him. All of us in the room have both big ideas about Kafka – prophet of modernity? Shakespeare of the twentieth century? gateway to the lost world of multi-ethnic Central Europe? – and our own niche interests that endlessly nuance and complicate these big ideas. Whether we can agree on how to place emphases in our visual story of Kafka's life, work and afterlife seems to hang in the balance.

'So you want people to come away knowing Kafka wrote in German?'

Yes, we do! The question of the exhibition designer working with us brings us back down to earth. Now: depending on how much you, the reader, knows about Kafka, and how you personally feel about the standards of cultural education, I can imagine a few different reactions you might be having right now. Perhaps you scoff impatiently and mutter to yourself, *everybody* knows Kafka wrote in German, and if they *don't*, then they're probably not interested in an exhibition of his precious manuscripts either! Or perhaps you gulp nervously and say, yes, yes, yes of course, all the while thinking to yourself: I must have known that, mustn't I?! Or you might say, ah, okay, he was a German writer, got it.

But that last one is not quite right, and grasping why it is not quite right is crucial to understanding not only Kafka and his work, but also the broader literary and cultural landscape in Europe in his time, and even the very fundamentals of how we think about literature and culture today. To explain what I mean, I will take this simple statement – 'Kafka was a German writer' – and reveal the irreducible complexity that lurks beneath it.

Kafka was not exactly German – or Austrian, or any other similar one-word label. His world cannot be neatly plotted on to the present map of German-speaking Europe. For most of his life, he was a subject of the Austro-Hungarian Empire, based near its northern edge, in Prague, a city that was then inhabited by various ethnic and religious groups. This included some German-speaking Jews like Kafka, but predominantly Czech-speaking Christians. In 1918, six years before Kafka's death, Prague became the capital of the Czechoslovak Republic.

Even calling Kafka a German-speaking Jew is more of an approximation than the full story. For one thing, like many in his family and wider milieu, he was not a practising Jew, or particularly interested in conventional religion at all, at least for most of his life. But he was fascinated by, and to some extent familiar with, the Yiddish language and culture of Eastern European Jews, learned some biblical Hebrew at school, and towards the end of his life made significant progress in modern Hebrew, even writing some short texts for practice. He also spoke Czech well – so well in fact that most linguists today would describe him as bilingual. He was brought up by a Czech-speaking maid, read Czech literature in school and beyond, regularly interacted with Czechs of various social classes in his work and private life, and sometimes would even use the Czech version of his name: František Kafka. And this is not to mention other classical and modern languages he learnt in various contexts, even if imperfectly: Latin, Greek, English, French and Italian.

There is a strong temptation to simplify stories like this. If you go to a bookshop or a library, even a highly specialised one, you will want to find Kafka on a shelf, and shelves need to be labelled to be found. So why can't we just say he was a German writer, since he wrote his literary works in German, and call it a day? One powerful argument for insisting on capturing the many layers of Kafka's linguistic identity is that it is not an exception, but the rule. Multilingualism – varying degrees of familiarity with two or more languages, often linguistically very distant ones, used in various social contexts – is how most people around the world operate, both today and throughout history. And having more than one version of one's name might seem unusual to monolingual Brits but will be familiar to most immigrants. In Poland, I spell my name with a diacritic – Wątroba – which changes the pronunciation. (And meaning: as much as I believe that others should be able to spell their names with diacritics and have their pronunciations respected, I cannot say that I much miss being called 'liver'!)

Similarly, Kafka was exposed not just to many different languages, but to many different varieties of German too. He met – and read – Germanophone people of various social classes from Prague, but also Vienna, Berlin, Munich, Leipzig and many other places. Older scholarship sometimes nevertheless made the claim that Kafka spoke and wrote a 'Prague German', understood as an isolated, impoverished dialect native to a diminishingly small community, and sought to explain the idiosyncrasies of his literature in this way, for example the supposed 'poverty' of his language.

But as linguist Marek Nekula's more recent, painstakingly detailed research has shown, this is a myth: while Kafka did sometimes describe his language as 'Prague German', and his written and – as far as we are able to reconstruct it – spoken German did contain some local peculiarities, those were often common to bigger regions, like Austria and southern Germany, and he often adjusted them in official letters or literary publications anyway. Kafka's stylistic choices might be described as lending his prose a stripped-down feel, but a similar quality in an ethnically German writer from Berlin might have been more readily described as, say, 'limpid'. In other words, while Kafka's local Prague context is in many ways central to the story of his life and work, as we will see in the next chapter, it is misleading to try to explain away the uniqueness of his writing by casting him as an isolated, provincial writer cut off from the literary universe of the wider world. Kafka was much more worldly, urbane even, than his readers often assume.

Ultimately, debates on Kafka's proficiency in his various languages rely on questionable assumptions about how we humans use language in the first place. It is not the case that insisting on Kafka's *multilingualism* is an unnecessary complication. Rather, calling Kafka a *German* writer is one. The innocuous little adjectives we are so used to seeing in front of the word 'writer' muddy the waters. They conflate nationality, ethnicity, language and sometimes religion – like in the case of the term 'Jewish' – and create an expectation, or express the implicit claim, that all literature is tied to a homogenous cultural formation, in its most orthodox form a nation that shares one ethnicity, religion and a standardised language. But such homogenous cultural formations rarely exist and, if they do, it is usually as a result of specific policies, especially in education, as well as much discrimination or even violence.

This was the case with Kafka too. Because of various historical developments, German was the language of social prestige among Jewish people living in Prague, so Kafka's parents sent him to a German-speaking school, even though as a small child he spoke Czech as much as – if not more than – German. For similar reasons, German as a literary language carried more cultural cachet than Czech, let alone Yiddish or Hebrew, and gave Kafka access to a much bigger and more prestigious literary market. Peter Zusi, a literary scholar interested in Kafka's Czech contemporaries, proposes a thought experiment: can we imagine Kafka gaining the same global fame had he written all his texts in Czech? The answer is likely no, for reasons that have nothing to do with the capacity of the Czech language for aesthetic value, but everything to do with the size and international prestige of the Czech literary scene at the time, cultural standing of translators from Czech, and so on.

A Tale of Many Plaques

We can trace the complexity and nuance of Kafka's linguistic and cultural identity exceptionally well by looking at a series of objects that might seem dull at first glance, but in fact hold intriguing clues as to how Kafka was perceived by various national and ethnic groups over the years: the many commemorative plaques erected in the decades since his death.

It all started with Kafka's gravestone in the New Jewish Cemetery in Prague, a striking concrete block in the shape of a crystal, designed by a local architect upon Kafka's death. The inscription on the gravestone is in *Hebrew* and gives his Hebrew name – Anschel – but starts with his name written out in *German*: Dr. Franz Kafka. It is not obvious that it would be in German: after all, Kafka's parents had two obituaries published for their son, one in German (for Dr. Franz Kafka) and one in Czech (for Dr. František Kafka). The fact that his doctoral title is included in all three texts – he was a Doctor of Law – serves as a subtle reminder of Kafka's socialisation in the *Austro-Hungarian* Empire with its famous obsession with titles and a rigid social hierarchy.

Against Kafka's gravestone, on which Hebrew inscriptions for both his parents were added when they died in the early 1930s, a smaller plaque is propped up, commemorating his three sisters, who were all murdered in Nazi concentration camps. It is entirely in *Czech* and describes Kafka as a 'famous *Prague Jewish* writer' (my italics). On the opposite wall, there is one more plaque, this time commemorating Max Brod; put up by the Jewish religious community of Prague, it describes Brod – in *Czech* – as a *Prague* writer and propagator of *Czech* culture abroad. It does not mention that, like Kafka, Brod wrote in *German*. Terms like 'German' or 'Austrian' are in fact entirely absent from these three commemorative plaques at the New Jewish Cemetery in Prague.

Meanwhile, on a house in Berlin in which Kafka lived for a few months in the last year of his life, there are two very different plaques. One, at the front, in white marble, was put in by the Republic of *Austria*, and describes Kafka as *Austrian*. Around the corner, there is another one, in blackened brass; put in by a post-war *German* council for the arts, it refrains from naming Kafka's nationality or ethnicity altogether. The most recent addition to this family is a plastic information board put up next to a rotating Kafka head, David Černý's outdoor sculpture installed in Prague in 2014.

It describes Kafka (in Czech, but an imperfect English translation is appended) as a '*Czech* writer of *Jewish* descent origin [sic] who wrote in *German*, born and lived [sic] in *Prague*' (again, my italics). Note that even this long and cumbersome label does not tell the full story, since it does not mention that for most of his life Kafka was a subject of the Austro-Hungarian Empire.

So what is the takeaway here? We need to free Kafka from our desire to simplify and contain him within a familiar label, not only because these are inescapably inaccurate and misleading, but also because – as we are about to see – the experience of evading simple labels was central to the formation of Kafka's literary imagination. More broadly, the understanding of national identity in early twentieth-century Europe was – at least in some ways – less entrenched than it is today. What it meant to be German and who could count as such, in particular, was still far from settled, and even gained a special designation: 'the German Question'.

The German word for 'German', 'Deutsch', comes from the ancient term for 'people', used to distinguish speakers of Germanic languages from those who used Romance or Celtic languages. Between the Middle Ages and the Napoleonic Wars, so for nearly 1,000 years, there existed the Holy Roman Empire of the German Nation, which covered huge swathes of Europe: at one point, this political unit contained what is now Germany, Austria, Switzerland, almost all of Benelux, as well as parts of eastern France, northern Italy, western Poland and more. In 1848, the first serious attempt was made to create a unified German nation state, but it was short lived, and the question of exactly which lands and peoples should be part of this state was hotly debated. For example, Jews were granted equal rights to Christians, but this did not put an end to discriminatory practices across many of the German territories. Another contested issue was whether the Austro-Hungarian Empire should be part of the new German nation state. Some favoured the so-called 'Small Germany', which would not include Austria, while others advocated for the 'Great Germany', with Austria – whose German name, 'Österreich', literally means 'Eastern realm' – at its south-eastern edge; another fringe option, sometimes referred to as 'Great Austria', was to include not just Austria, but all Habsburg lands. After much debate and conflict, it was the 'Small Germany' solution that prevailed when the German Empire was proclaimed in 1871.

But this did not settle the issue once and for all. During Kafka's life, the term 'Kulturnation' was coined for the idea that being German had less to do with political statehood and more with shared cultural heritage. It followed that you could be German without being a citizen of or living in the German Empire. The great paradox of the idea of the 'Kulturnation' is that it can be taken in radically different directions: for example, it could be – and was – used to provide an avenue of identification for German-speaking Jews, or to exclude them from the imagined community of the nation, mainly because what constitutes a 'shared cultural heritage' is so fraught.

The choice of national, ethnic, linguistic and religious descriptors applied to Kafka has always been fraught and complex too, as various groups have sought to commemorate his legacy over the years. I think about this irreducible complexity of Kafka's identity, how important it is to normalise it, and how the English-speaking world in particular seems inhospitable to it, as I huddle up in a decidedly too thin coat on an unexpectedly blustery April day in Prague. I am waiting for Černý's 'Hlava Franze Kafky', or 'Franz Kafka's Head', to commence its next half-hourly rotation.

Despite the wealth of places that were significant to Kafka all around Prague, this huge installation – over ten metres tall and weighing nearly forty tonnes – has been placed in a small, rather unattractive square that did not play any role in his life. It is there because it was funded by the generic modern shopping centre it sits in front of. I am now surrounded by a sizeable crowd that has formed around the head, which is made up of forty curving strips of polished stainless steel with kilometres of invisible cable tucked underneath. Finally, the performance begins: individual strips start to move in a complex choreography, first fast, then slower, a quarter of an hour of mesmerising movement, Kafka's metal head bizarrely dissolving into chunks of metal only to come together again seconds or minutes later.

The sculpture is garish and all its polished surface reflects is the shopping centre and the surrounding dull little square. But as much as I have been primed to dislike it, I cannot look away. This incessant decomposition of Kafka into separate elements, jutting out in all directions, only to seamlessly meld into one giant head again at the end, is not a bad visual metaphor for our continuing trouble grasping his identity. We might be accustomed to thinking of all the different aspects of his self as separate or even incompatible, but that is just how they appear to us: in fact, they easily slot into one another to form a perfect whole.

Circus Rider on Two Horses

Having written the previous sentence, I sat back and let out a satisfied sigh. You will have to grant me this little moment of utopian possibility. But in fact Kafka's composite identity did cause him trouble throughout his life. In 1916, he studied reviews of *The Metamorphosis*, which had come out the previous year. In between their *two* engagements, Kafka reported in a letter to Felice Bauer that one review – published in the very prestigious literary magazine *Die neue Rundschau* (the *New Review*), based in Berlin, where Bauer lived – described his writing as possessing an 'urdeutsch', 'primevally' or 'essentially' German quality, while another – written by Brod for Martin Buber's monthly *Der Jude* (the *Jew*) – counted his works among the 'jüdischsten Dokumente unserer Zeit', 'the most Jewish documents of our time'. 'Won't you tell me what I really am', Franz pleads with Felice, and goes on to answer his own question: 'A difficult case. Am I a circus rider on 2 horses? Alas, I am no rider, but lie prostrate on the ground.'

This little comment is pregnant with implications. As unworkable as the position of the circus rider, or rather non-rider, sounds, it is hard to resist the impression that in these two lines Kafka gives us an odd little insight into the fount of his creativity. His literary texts are full of horses, riders, circuses, striking images reminiscent of a 'circus rider on two horses', and sliding paradoxes along the lines of a rider who turns out to be no rider at all, but rather lands flat on his face. This remark in a letter to Bauer in fact resembles Kafka's microfiction – extremely short literary pieces, often resembling fables, parables, aphorisms or even Buddhist koans – whether the early examples collected in his first ever published book, *Betrachtung* (*Meditation*, 1912), or the later ones, written in 1917–18 and known as *The Zürau Aphorisms*. Here is an example of the former, titled 'Wish to Become a Red Indian':

> Oh to be a Red Indian, ready in an instant, riding a swift horse, aslant in the air, thundering again and again over the thundering earth, until you let the spurs go, for there weren't any spurs, until you cast off the reins, for there weren't any reins, and you scarcely saw the land ahead of you as close-cropped scrub, being already without horse's neck and horse's head!

This miniature fantasy projects the narrator's burning desire for freedom on to an imagined Indigenous person, identified by means of an old-fashioned European term. (Kafka's German term is 'Indianer', so it is not based in unscientific and outdated colour terminology for race like the English translation, but it still reflects a European optic, external to the world of Indigenous peoples.) What connects this little vignette to Kafka's remark in the letter to Bauer is that both draw an implicit parallel between horse-riding and personal identity on the one hand, and the act of writing on the other.

In the letter, Kafka meditates on the authorial identity that his readers project on to his texts, and whether he can survive under the weight of their expectations. In *Meditation*, the text unfurls in one restless, feverish sentence, unfinished in the German, where it begins with 'wenn . . . doch', 'if only': a wish which cannot be fulfilled. An impression of the rider's breakneck speed is created through a

56

quick succession of short clauses. But a mental image of this rider on a faraway continent is evoked in the first half of the sentence only to be then dismantled, bit by bit, clause by clause: no spurs, no reins, barely any land ahead, the horse headless, neckless, with the rider about to become 'no rider' too, as in Kafka's letter. Time and again Kafka's writing draws our attention to how quickly identities can shift and change, transforming moment to moment. A horse and a rider become an absence of everything that defined them; an ordinary man wakes up a monstrous cockroach.

Here is another example, the very first aphorism in a collection edited and published by Brod in 1931:

The true way goes over a rope which is not stretched at any great height but just above the ground. It seems more designed to make people stumble than to be walked upon.

No circus here, and no horses – and yet a similar image, of a person carefully keeping their balance in a challenging position, whether on a tightrope or on the backs of two horses; but in the blink of an eye, the text shifts without warning, and we are invited to instead picture somebody falter. Or, as in the letter to Bauer, somebody already 'prostrate on the ground'. All three texts seem to belong to the same family – of deep metaphysical reflections on existential precarity, on our relationship to the world through which we move so unsteadily, worked out in a language of horse riding, circuses and tightropes.

Even though few of Kafka's works were published during his lifetime, and those that did come out did not sell well, they were widely reviewed. Granted, many of these reviews were written by Kafka's friends, or by Brod's contacts, or – as we have seen – by Brod himself. But others came from critics who did not know Kafka personally and appeared in newspapers and magazines across German-speaking Europe: not just in the German-language press in Prague, but also in Vienna and Berlin, as well as Leipzig – where Kafka's publisher, Kurt Wolff, was based – Munich, Frankfurt, Stuttgart and Bern. Many reviews were positive, some even deferential.

But neither his reviewers nor Kafka himself could conceive of a cultural landscape in which 'German' and 'Jewish' are not antitheses but two aspects of one person's experience – even though that is exactly what Kafka's works represent. As anti-Semitic sentiment was on the rise in interwar Germany, one was more likely to instead come across a sneer like this one, published in 1921 in a right-wing Berlin paper as a comment on a long essay about Kafka in the prestigious *Neue Rundschau*: 'it has been a while since *German* writers were last discussed in there' – as opposed to *Jewish* ones, presumably. For this commentator, Kafka was decidedly *not* German.

Such a critic would struggle to understand that Kafka could not only be both German and Jewish, but that his lived experience was even more capacious. Had Kafka quoted more extensively from the review in *Die neue Rundschau* in his letter to Bauer, he could have mentioned that it discussed his work alongside Gustav Meyrink and Kasimir Edschmid. The former wrote *The Golem*, a fantastical novel inspired by legends of a rabbi carrying out alchemical experiments in Prague's medieval Jewish ghetto. To the reviewer, the first name of the latter – Kasimir – 'seems to also suggest something Slavic'. The review continues: 'A literary centre has formed there, which is very stimulating for a literary geographer . . . these three fantasists stand at the southern end of the German pendulum.' So Kafka is not just German and Jewish: he is apparently also marked by the proximity of Slavdom, Europe's mysterious south-eastern edge.

But in the case of Kasimir Edschmid, this was an illusion. It was a pseudonym adopted by Eduard Schmid, who was born in Switzerland and spent most of his life in Germany. In his own review of Kafka's *Metamorphosis*, Edschmid writes about Prague with its new 'mysterious', 'miraculous' and 'spiritual' literature thus: 'It is still Europe here, still Germany, but we are already at the border of Asia. Here begins the Orient.' Both his own enthusiastic reverie and his critics' musings evoke a centuries-long, clichéd narrative widespread across the German-speaking lands, according to which Slavic peoples were fundamentally different, wild and mysterious. Whether Edschmid was aware of it or not, in most inflections of this narrative, 'different, wild and mysterious' also meant 'culturally inferior' – and by extension in dire need of Germanic colonisation. As Kristin Kopp's fascinating book *Germany's Wild East: Constructing Poland as Colonial Space* shows, this often led to racist prejudices against Asians being collapsed with an anti-Slavic sentiment; during Kafka's lifetime, Eastern Europe would sometimes be dubbed 'Half-Asia'. Edschmid's comments about Prague as a gateway to 'Asia' and 'the Orient' fit into this broader pattern.

Kafka's experience of cultural diversity certainly helped shape his writing, but the desire to explain the startling originality of his work through his proximity to the Slavic lands reflects longstanding, exoticising stereotypes about the region. I am more sympathetic to the somewhat different reasoning of an Austrian reviewer of Jewish-Hungarian heritage, written for another Berlin newspaper, this time about Kafka's earlier *Meditation*: 'Such depressing (and yet brilliant) books are only written in states without a violently expansionist politics.' He goes on: 'What Kafka says sounds like something whispered by one of the few gentle, quiet characters pressed against the wall, of the kind that can no longer be found anywhere but in the kingdoms and lands represented by the Austrian Imperial Council.' One reason why Kafka became Kafka is that he happened to be born in the margins of the German-speaking world, in the provinces of a decaying, impotent empire which would disappear from the map during his lifetime, rather than in the powerful German Empire intent on rivalling Europe's most belligerent colonial nations.

A German Education

Kafka's sensibility was fine-tuned to such musings. Travelling with Brod in Switzerland, he jotted down what he called a 'patriotic statistic': 'the size of Switzerland if it were laid out flat'. Its area would then surely be greater than that of the German Empire, explained Brod, who also noted down this little joke. A few years earlier, when Brod mentioned Kafka's name at the end of an article about exciting new writing in German, even though no works by him had yet been published, Kafka responded that clearly no German reader would be desperate enough to read to the end of such an article, and so would not learn his name. 'But it is another matter with Germans abroad,' he wrote in a letter to Brod, 'in the Baltic Provinces, for example, or still better in America, or most of all in the German colonies; for the forlorn German reads his magazine through and through. Thus the centre of my fame must be Dar es Salaam, Ujiji, Windhoek.' Even though these were clearly not meant as serious comments, they still show how sensitive Kafka was to the subtle gradations of the power dynamic in the German-speaking world.

One consequence of this dynamic was that the literary education he received at school tended towards the conservative and the nationalistic. In his written school-leaving exam in German, rather than holding forth about any literary works, Kafka had to describe the advantages of Austria's geopolitical situation: that was the kind of topic that his school education was supposed to teach him about. But literature was covered in the curriculum too, and here Austrian authors were not exactly absent, but decidedly less emphasised than the greats of the traditional *German* national canon: Lessing, Goethe, Schiller and Kleist.

But let us stop and consider what sort of nation this canon in fact represented. Lessing grew up at the edge of Lusatia, a region which today is split between Germany and Poland and has long been inhabited by Sorbs, a Slavic ethnic group with its own distinctive linguistic and cultural identity. He wrote his famous aesthetic treatise *Laocoön* while working in Breslau – now Wrocław in Poland, but over the centuries variously under Polish, Czech, Habsburg, Prussian and German rule. Kleist was born and studied in Frankfurt an der Oder, a city whose eastern part became part of Poland after 1945, the river in its name now serving as the national border. Like Lessing and Kleist, Goethe and Schiller wrote their works decades before the unification of Germany in 1871, which simply did not exist as a nation state for most of European history, even if national sentiments were present in some form in the writing of these authors. Strategically selected and appropriately interpreted works of these men were later used to construct a canon that was meant to carefully delineate and police the boundaries between the German nation and its 'Others', such as Jews and Slavs, even – or especially – in the face of their close proximity.

No wonder that Kafka found it difficult to embrace the label of an 'urdeutsch' writer, as seen in his letter to Bauer. The focus of his German lessons at school was also on poetry and drama, not prose, which had long been seen as an inferior literary mode – but that was precisely the form that he adopted as his. This disconnect between German literature as it was taught to him and as he practised it himself continued at university. Kafka attended lectures by August Sauer, who struck chauvinistic tones in an attempt to assert the superiority of German literature and culture over its Czech, or more generically 'Slavic' counterpart. Kafka could not stand it and stopped attending the lectures.

But he did value the writings of such German classics as Goethe and Kleist highly. Many early reviewers compared his works to Kleist's novellas, and in 1912 Kafka relished an opportunity to follow in Goethe's footsteps on a trip to Weimar and take a look at some of his manuscripts, even if he was put off by the pompous name of Goethe's house – 'Goethe-Nationalmuseum'. Kafka was there eighty years after Goethe's death – an amount of time comparable to that which now separates us from Kafka's own death. Upon realising this, I eagerly immersed myself in the diary entries that record this trip in search of further clues for how Kafka approached his canonical predecessor, in the hope that we might have something to learn from it as we face the canonical nimbus of Kafka himself.

But he seems to have spent most of his time and energy in Weimar trying to pick up the sixteen-year-old daughter of the caretaker of Goethe's house, nearly half his age and called – of all names – Grete, like the young heroine of Goethe's *Faust*, who is seduced by the titular scholar with tragic consequences. In his diary, Kafka hastily jots down his impressions: 'Goethe House. Reception rooms. Glimpse of the study and bedroom. Sad sight reminiscent of dead grandfathers. That garden growing continuously since Goethe's death. The beech tree darkening his study.' Innocent enough impressions, familiar from my own visit to Weimar many decades later. But then: 'She had already run past us with her little sister when we were sitting at the foot of the stairs. In my memory the plaster cast of a greyhound at the foot of the stairs is associated with this running. Then we saw her again in the Juno room, then while looking out from the garden room. Many other times I thought I heard her footsteps and her voice.' There is no way to know what exactly happened between Kafka and Grete; Brod called Kafka's flirtation 'successful'. I am left discombobulated by this story, which feels like Kafka's unsavoury re-enactment of Goethe's *Faust*.

On a Train Across the German Lands

In between two academic terms, with the story of Kafka's

trip to Weimar fresh in my memory, I am free to set out on my own journey in search of 'German' Kafka. But how to go about it? Where to find him? As we have already established, Kafka is perhaps the most famous German-language writer of all time, but he lived on the very margins of what we usually think of as German-speaking Europe. Still, he was enamoured with Berlin, where he stayed several times – including in 1923 and 1924, shortly before his death. He also travelled to other cities and towns around Europe, always by train. And so, on a chilly day in early spring, I too catch a train, first from Oxford to London, then from London to Paris, and finally from Paris to Zurich; I then take a sleeper train from there to Berlin. From Berlin, it is easy to travel on: to Prague, Vienna or . . . Marbach am Neckar.

That is where the biggest literary archive in Germany is located: a sleepy town north of Stuttgart, chiefly known as the birthplace of Friedrich Schiller. Its many literary treasures include a significant number of Kafka's manuscripts, some co-owned with the Bodleian Library in Oxford. But Kafka had no connection to the place itself, or this part of Germany at all. Many of his manuscripts spent decades locked up in a bank vault in Zurich. That city Kafka did visit, in 1911, accompanied by Brod. I decide to make a stop there too. Although he only spent some ten hours in Zurich, such are the depths of Kafkology that we have an extremely detailed record of his time there, based on his and Brod's diaries – a painstaking reconstruction of their route and various activities, adumbrated with historical maps and photographs.

Perhaps the most haunting detail is this: from the train station, Kafka and Brod walked down the Bahnhofstrasse, then and now one of the most luxurious shopping streets in Europe, lined with boutiques, cafés and banks. It does have an unnervingly polished, artificial look – and so, apparently, it did over a century ago. James Joyce, who lived in Zurich during the First World War and wrote most of *Ulysses* there, is supposed to have once said that the street was so clean that one could slurp minestrone off the pavement. In 1911, Kafka admired the buildings of two banks on Bahnhofstrasse: Credit Suisse (back then called Eidgenössische Creditanstalt) and Schweizerische Nationalbank. A few hours later, he was back on the train and continuing his journey across Switzerland, which would culminate in one of his first sanatorium stays – years before he was diagnosed with the tuberculosis that would ultimately kill him, when it still seemed an innocuous respite from the obligations of work and everyday life. Little did he know that just two years after his visit to Zurich, the banks he marvelled at would be outshone by a new seat of the UBS on Bahnhofstrasse, the bank which would end up housing most of his manuscripts for several decades.

Kafka's diary from that year reads like a messy, unfiltered catalogue of various people he met on his travels, starting – in January – with a gaunt man in his train compartment who ate sausage ('a very thin passenger was wolfing down ham, bread, and two sausages, the skins of which he kept scraping with a knife until they were transparent') while Kafka watched the man's enormous penis bulging in his trousers. No English reader would have been familiar with this unappetising image, though, since the only English translation of his diaries available until 2023 omitted this sentence. Ross Benjamin's brand-new retranslation fills in the gap: 'His apparently sizable member makes a large bulge in his pants.'

While at the sanatorium, one new acquaintance in particular catches Kafka's attention. It is a young Jewish man from Cracow, who has just come back from a two-year stint working in America. ('He had long, curly hair, only occasionally ran his fingers through it, very bright eyes, a gently curving nose, hollows in his cheeks, a suit of American cut, a frayed shirt, falling socks.') Kafka thinks he can hear an English accent in his speech, English idioms creeping in too; they make his German 'unruhig' – 'unsettled', 'restless', like the dreams from which Gregor Samsa wakes to find himself transformed into a monstrous insect at the beginning of *The Metamorphosis*. This productive restlessness will soon drive Kafka to turn his chance encounter with a young emigrant from Cracow into literature: he will turn him into Karl Roßmann, the protagonist of *The Man who Disappeared*, a teenage Eastern European boy who travels to Kafka's strange, fictional 'Amerika' on his own, and struggles to find his way around this unfamiliar new country.

Travel between Eastern Europe, the German-speaking Central Europe and the English-speaking West; chance encounters with strangers; Kafka, who makes literature out of them; the century that lies between his life and ours; and the shadow of a young man from Cracow, who mixes German and English as he speaks, the man who becomes Kafka's immigrant hero Karl. I feel like I have found a foothold in Kafka's world. And one last thing: 'Roßmann' means 'horseman'.

Vienna and Berlin

Like the circus rider on two horses, this young man from Cracow is another figure who occupies the liminal space in which Kafka seemingly records his life but ends up transforming it into literature in the process: both fact and fiction. Here again it is the visceral encounter with a multi-layered cultural identity that gets Kafka's imagination going. And this is why in my search for Kafka I prefer to take the circuitous route: this is why I get off the train in places like Marbach and Zurich first, even if they do not seem to straightforwardly offer *the* key to Kafka's mental geography of German-speaking Europe. Such a route allows me to better appreciate the tensions, intricacies and power structures of Kafka's German universe, infinitely more complex than a simple dyad of Berlin and Vienna. (In Zurich, he marvelled with Brod at the local dialect: 'German poured out like lead.')

But now I should go for the big guns, should I not? Berlin and Vienna? Ach, Vienna. Kafka did not have much respect for what was for most of his life the imperial capital of his country, increasingly grinding to a halt as Habsburg bureaucracy reached gargantuan proportions in the years leading up to the First World War. His contempt was widespread at the time, with Vienna often explicitly or implicitly compared to Berlin – and coming up short: smaller, less progressive, less exciting. For Kafka, it was an 'absterbendes Riesendorf' – a 'decaying mammoth village', or literally a 'dying' one. What a cruel coincidence that Kafka himself ended up dying in a sanatorium in Kierling, just beyond the northern edge of the city, having studiously avoided travelling to Vienna unless absolutely necessary all his life. By the time he died there, he was a Czech citizen and Vienna was abroad. Today, tourists following in Kafka's footsteps can visit a reconstruction of the sanatorium room in which he died.

The initial plan in the last weeks of Kafka's life, though, was to send him to Davos in the Swiss Alps. This was the world's most famous town for tuberculosis sufferers on account of its many sanatoria, about to be immortalised in Thomas Mann's novel *The Magic Mountain*, which came out just a few months after Kafka's death. *The Magic Mountain* was and still is my favourite novel, so I was gratified to discover that Mann and Kafka read and admired each other's work.

The strange coincidence of Kafka's real-life death from tuberculosis and the publication of Mann's classic literary treatment of the disease feels symbolic, as though it were an unspoken but urgent message about the relative seriousness of life and literature. Kafka's seven-year-long, painful struggle with tuberculosis might cast unfavourable light on Mann's sophisticated novelisation of a seven-year-long retreat into a luxurious Swiss sanatorium. Many readers are drawn to Kafka precisely because of this impression of deeper authenticity, or immediacy of experience; Kafka's writing might lack Mann's polished elegance, but it offers other rewards.

I keep finding ways to look beyond Vienna when attempting to write about Kafka's experience of the city. Something similar actually happened to the man himself. In September 1913, Kafka travelled to Vienna on a work trip. He was supposed to attend the Second International Congress for Rescue Services and Accident Prevention, and he did – but another event was simultaneously vying for his attention:

the Eleventh Zionist Congress, first launched by Theodor Herzl in 1897 with the goal of promoting Jewish immigration to Palestine, met in Vienna at the same time. Kafka attended a few sessions of this congress too. Some of his friends thought of him as a Zionist, but, as I explain in Chapter Four, his attitude towards Zionism was much more complex. In a letter to Felice Bauer, he described the congress speeches as 'ergebnislos' – 'inconclusive', or 'barren of results'. Both before and after the congress he did consider the possibility of moving to Palestine, though; in the heart of Vienna, Kafka was listening to speeches about life elsewhere.

Now Berlin was something different. It was a cultural hotspot and huge metropolis, especially by early twentieth-century standards. In the 1920s, its population exceeded 4 million, which made it one of the largest cities worldwide, rivalled only by New York, London, Paris and Tokyo. Interestingly, while these four kept expanding and are now home to many more people than they were in the 1920s, Berlin has shrunk: it never fully recovered from the destruction of the Second World War and its population still has not reached the levels witnessed by Kafka. But in the 1920s, the population was growing rapidly, and Berlin was changing fast to accommodate it. Construction was going on all around the city, with modern technology used to erect new buildings and carry out infrastructure projects; public transport was playing an increasingly large role in everyday life; there were new shops with fancy display windows lit up with new electric lighting. The old and the new coexisted in the city at that point: in the streets, electric trams would be seen alongside horse-drawn carriages, and flashy shop windows

and technologically advanced transportation and communication systems alongside numerous families struggling to
survive, with no jobs, stuck in inadequate housing in poor
neighbourhoods, not benefitting from the economic growth
celebrated on the streets of central Berlin.

Kafka first went to Berlin for a short trip in 1910; he
would return many times, have vivid dreams about it, fan-
tasise about moving there permanently for years, twice get
engaged to Felice Bauer who lived there, and finally make it
in 1923, when his health was already in serious decline and
the German capital was in the throes of unprecedented infla-
tion. It was not quite the exciting, relentlessly modern Berlin
of cabarets, avant-garde art, and Weimar politics. Kafka
stayed in three different apartments in suburban areas in the
south-west of the city, which had only just been formally
made part of Berlin. He did occasionally venture into the
city centre, but found it tiring, loud and unpleasant, especially on account of his progressing illness. But even during
his earlier visits, Kafka never felt at ease hanging out in fash-
ionable coffeehouses with popular bohemian literati of the
day, despite his ongoing fantasy of a life as a full-time writer.

Kafka ended up living in Berlin for just six months, but
his stay there has exercised the imaginations of readers for
many decades now, for several reasons. First of all, for a
writer who spent almost all of his life up to that point within
the 2 km radius of central Prague, but who so often berated
his hometown and fantasised about moving elsewhere, this
final, hopeless act of relocating to Berlin is deeply moving.
And not only did Kafka finally move, but he also finally
moved in with a woman. Well, not quite: Dora Diamant, an
activist working with Jewish refugee children from Poland,

where she was born herself, and whom Kafka met less than two months before his move, never formally shared a house with him, but took on the role of his caretaker and visited him almost daily. None of Kafka's previous relationships, including his three engagements, ever brought him into such physical proximity with a woman.

In Berlin, Kafka continued writing, mostly letters and short stories, which obliquely reflected curious details from his everyday life in the city. But perhaps his most notorious piece of writing from Berlin is the one that we cannot read: his children's novel.

Kafka's Doll

Now, whether this novel really did exist, we will never know for certain, but Dora Diamant's story about it does not sound implausible, and there is no strong reason to doubt it. On one of their frequent walks in a local park, Kafka and Diamant encountered an upset little girl. What was wrong, Kafka asked? She had lost her doll, the girl answered tearfully. To comfort her, Kafka came up with a little story on the spot. The doll had gone travelling, which he happened to know because she had sent him a letter. He would bring it to the park the following day.

Kafka went home and penned the first of some twenty letters, full of humorous details, in which the doll gave an account of her adventures, culminating in a wedding and the decision to settle down away from her Berlin home. Kafka would bring a new letter to the park every day for 'at least three weeks' and read it out to the girl, Diamant explained. He took this task seriously: 'He set to work as earnestly as if to write literature,' she reminisced. That was how he approached all of his writing: 'He was always in this agitated frame of mind as soon as he sat down at his desk, even if all he had to write was a letter or postcard.' Even, or especially, if it was to come from a fictional doll.

If this story is true, Kafka wrote an epistolary children's novel in the last year of his life. Did he indeed adopt 'the language of dolls', as writer Anthony Rudolf put it? An attractive proposition, and one that makes intuitive sense: Kafka's surviving texts often have something of a fairy-tale quality anyway, in that they feature countless sentient, intelligent creatures who are not quite human, defy traditional logic, and are usually written in an – often deceptively – simple language. Many people who knew Kafka also remembered him as particularly friendly towards children, or even childlike himself, long into adulthood. Last but not least, what is so touching about the doll's story is that it sounds like Kafka's own biography. According to Diamant's summary, the doll 'had had enough of forever living in the same family'; she wished for a 'change of air'. Kafka expressed similar sentiments about his own family again and again, until he finally acted upon them and moved to Berlin. It is tempting to imagine that he reflected on this long-awaited change in the medium of a children's book.

But even if Diamant – who, when Kafka met her, was working with Jewish refugee children from Eastern Europe – invented this story, it is a particularly attractive one because it captures a side of Kafka's character that long remained invisible in dominant critical accounts of his life and work. Quite literally so.

Consider the covers of two influential books about

Kafka. Marthe Robert, one of the first French scholars of Kafka, to whom Diamant told the story of the lost doll in the 1950s, in the 1970s published a book titled *Seul, comme Franz Kafka* – or, in an English translation, *As Lonely as Franz Kafka*. On the cover of the French edition, there is a familiar photograph of Kafka: a bowler hat over a wistful gaze, a forlorn hand folded on his lap. Or is it? Have a look at the cover of another book, this time an English translation of *Franz Kafka. Bilder aus seinem Leben – Franz Kafka: Pictures of a Life*, by Klaus Wagenbach, one of the most distinguished scholars of Kafka. It features the same photograph, but cropped differently so that, on Kafka's right, we can see a dog. In fact, Kafka is patting its furry back. Not so forlorn after all? Well, it gets even better once we examine the original photograph. It turns out that next to the dog sits a young, laughing woman, cheerfully patting its back, just like her male companion, the 'lonely' Franz Kafka.

The woman has been identified as Juliane Szokoll, a bar waitress from Prague, who went by the name Hansi, and with whom Kafka had an affair in his early twenties, according to Brod. This is an example of editing Kafka's social relationships out of his life, which can be done through a selective focus on some passages from his diaries and letters over others, overemphasis on some themes in his novels and stories over others, or, as here, cropping photographs so that Kafka appears as a solitary, pensive gentleman rather than a man about town, a friend or even lover, someone who liked and was kind to dogs – the story the photograph as a whole tells us.

Now, compare all this to another image: Kafka smiling gregariously, hands clasped over nonchalantly crossed legs, sitting on a park bench next to a little girl, the pair exchanging knowing glances over a pile of letters. This is the cover of *Kafka and the Doll*, Larissa Theule's recent children's book illustrated by Rebecca Green. It is fiction – but this version of Kafka captures a side of his personality that has been often edited out, and so can act as a useful counterweight to the image of a brooding, lone man glancing at us from the covers of innumerable other books.

Readers on Standby

Another important lesson from the tale of Kafka and the doll? Like many other stories in this book, it shows us a procession of readers who are very far from just passive recipients of the writer's word, but rather deeply emotionally invested, and in some cases even ready to step in and take up the pen themselves. *Kafka and the Doll* is one of more than a dozen books and stories – alongside a Polish puppet show, especially fitting since it is called 'dolls' theatre' in Polish – which have grown out of various readers' fascination with the story of Kafka's missing novel about the travelling doll, authored in countries ranging from Germany and Switzerland to France, Italy and Spain, from the Netherlands and Great Britain to Poland and Czechia, and from the United States to Argentina.

If Kafka really had written an epistolary novel to comfort a little girl in a Berlin park, then she was a reader who prompted the writing in the first place: a reader on standby, in place before the story even takes shape, both inspiring and co-creating the literary text. A 'privileged little girl, the only reader of Kafka's most beautiful book', as writer César Aira called her in a moving essay in *El País*. And do not forget Dora Diamant, the woman so invested in both Kafka and alleviating the suffering of children that she either kept this story alive for other readers of Kafka, or possibly even made up or at least embellished this apocryphal episode – in which case she would be another reader-turned-writer, telling a fictional story of her beloved writer's last novel. Whether or not the story is true, it has been repeatedly retold and ended up sparking not only numerous literary versions of the events recounted by Diamant, but also of the epistolary novel itself.

But what about Kafka's actual manuscript? Supposing it really existed, could we not find it? There have been several attempts over the years. Articles in the local and even national press urged the residents of Steglitz, the district surrounding the park where the encounter with the little girl supposedly took place, to go through old papers in their attics in search of Kafka's last novel. At the turn of the millennium, Mark Harman, an Irish-American translator of Kafka, spent a year in Berlin at a prestigious academic fellowship. He dedicated much of his time in the German capital to trying to track down the putative bundle of letters from Kafka *aka* the doll. He did manage to locate and talk to the elderly daughter of one of Kafka's Berlin landlords. But the manuscript was not found then – or since – and it seems unlikely that it will ever surface again.

And yet smaller discoveries still await. In 2012, a local tourist guide who specialises in Kafka-themed walks in Steglitz reported in a local newspaper how, on one of these, her group stopped in a small pub opposite the site of one of the houses where Kafka stayed for a couple of months that fateful autumn of 1923. The house no longer stands, replaced by a post-war block of flats, and no photos of the original house were preserved. Or so the guide believed – until it turned out that the proprietor of the pub, a long-standing family business, had one. Yet another little trace of Kafka in Berlin.

We have now met a whole host of writers, critics, translators and locals who have followed in Kafka's footsteps in Berlin on an indefatigable search for a children's book he might or might not have written. But in this chapter we also encountered a well-educated veteran of the First World War who comes back from the front seemingly unscathed but loses his bearings when confronted with Kafka's enigmatic tale of a man turned into a verminous insect, as well as a world-famous scientist who feels compelled to unleash a Twitterstorm because over one hundred years later this very same story bugs him no end. They all join our assorted cast of Kafka's readers: Malcolm Pasley, the British baronet who brought Kafka's manuscripts to Oxford in his own car and employed investigative skills to prepare a critical edition of his works; the curator at the Bodleian Library who cannot actually read Kafka's manuscripts as she does not read German, but nevertheless treats them like saintly relics to preserve them for future generations; and numerous readers across Britain and beyond who turned to Kafka in times of Brexit and coronavirus to try to find a way through these crises.

What is it that drove and still drives so many different readers of Kafka to chase his shadow, whether in Prague and Berlin during his own life, or now, across time and space? Part of the answer that I have been outlining so far is the disorientation caused by Kafka's writing. It might be tempting for readers to interpret this disorientation as a failure of the text, as both Siegfried Wolff and Richard Dawkins came close to doing. But for many readers, like those reading *The Metamorphosis* to make sense of the coronavirus pandemic, the feeling of disorientation becomes a crucial part of their experience of the text. These are not reassuring stories that order the chaos of human life into coherent plots which either end well or at least follow an intelligible chain of cause and effect. Instead, Kafka's tales evoke such traditional narrative structures of understanding, but fill them in with strange, chaotic, disorienting events that are difficult to make sense of, and in this way vindicate the anxiety of real life, which rarely lives up to the coherence of realist literature.

But this is not the end of the story. There is another, parallel layer of complexity in Kafka: the identity of the author himself, which often was and still often is misunderstood or simplified, both by his contemporaries and his readers today. We have met reviewers who read Kafka's books as they first came out and could not quite agree on the source of the essential strangeness of his imagination, or how to even place this German-language writer from a Jewish family living in Prague among Czech friends and colleagues. We have seen how this uncertainty or discomfort surrounding Kafka's composite identity has continued to this day, with a merry procession of commemorative plaques variously describing Kafka as German, Jewish, Czech or Austrian.

We have seen Kafka himself reflect on this instability in a letter to Felice Bauer, where he imagines himself as a circus rider on two horses: seemingly out of thin air he creates a startling vignette which reads very much like some of his famous parables and aphorisms. Similarly, a casual meeting with a stranger – a Jewish man from Poland, who speaks German with an American accent – sets off Kafka's imagination, remarkably sensitive to individuals who – like Kafka himself – do not fit the mould. This man will be transformed into the immigrant protagonist of one of Kafka's three novels and given the name of Roßmann – none other than 'horseman'.

What the last two examples show is that those two types of disorientating complexity – of Kafka's identity and his writing – are connected: one led to and was reflected in the other. By embracing Kafka's complexity, both in terms of his texts and his identity, we can better understand the complexity of our own history, and present: the dangers of trying to pin things and people down, of neatly sorting them into convenient, immediately intelligible, but ultimately artificial and misleading categories. It is a lesson in nuance, which we badly need in our world today.

I contemplate our ongoing collective search for Kafka on a bench in the rose garden of the very park where, according to Diamant, the two of them met the little girl who had lost her doll. The layout of the park has changed since the 1920s, but the rose garden remains. And the visitors' demographic has not changed much either: a children's choir puts in an energetic practice opposite my bench, threatening to slide into horrifying cacophony at any moment. A train of jackdaws flies overhead. I smile – did you know that the Czech word for jackdaw is 'kavka'?

3

Prague

Czech Kafka

Into the Kafkorium

Despite having been born in Cracow, not far from Prague, where Kafka lived for most of his life, I had never visited the Czech capital until I took up my search for Kafka in earnest. Like many Eastern Europeans, growing up I was encouraged to take much more interest in what lay further afield in the West. I had also lazily assumed that Prague could not be much different from Cracow. After all, the foundation of both these cities is shrouded in legends about mythical Slavic rulers, and each gained prominence in the Middle Ages as a royal seat of a powerful Central European dynasty with an imposing castle and cathedral on a hill overlooking a major river, surrounded by rapidly growing towns inhabited by Slavs, Germans and Jews. Both Prague and Cracow were eventually incorporated into the Austrian Empire and remained part of it until its dissolution in 1918; later both were invaded by Nazi Germany, and were subsequently under Soviet control until 1989. Today they are beautifully restored, thanks in no small part to funds from the European Union, which both the Czech Republic and Poland joined in

2004, and are increasingly popular with international tourists. Polish and Czech, the two biggest members of the West Slavic language group, are so closely related that in some contexts they are mutually intelligible. In short, sitting on a train from Berlin to Prague I feel pretty confident that I know what to expect.

But as soon as I get off the train and step into the awe-inspiring, high-ceilinged, art nouveau gem of a station building, I realise that I have got it wrong. In its scale and grandeur, Prague resembles Paris more than Cracow. Its townhouses are taller and more imposing, its cafés more spacious and cosmopolitan. The Charles Bridge and the National Theatre can easily rival Pont Alexandre III and Opéra Garnier in Paris. Grand Hotel Europa in the famous Wenceslas Square boasts what simply must be the most charming art nouveau façade anywhere on the continent. Like all these landmarks, the hotel was already there in Kafka's time: in fact, he gave a rare public reading in what was then known as Hotel Erzherzog Stephan (Archduke Stephen). I will be taking in all these sights with a certain degree of disbelief over the next few days but already, on that very first evening, before I even get to my accommodation, I manage to articulate the source of my cognitive dissonance: the mental image of Prague I have formed over the years by reading Kafka, and reading about him, was of a suffocating, provincial town that any urbane, cultivated person would be desperate to leave as soon as possible. 'Prague doesn't let go', Kafka proclaimed in a letter to a friend as early as 1902; 'This old crone has claws.' 'Leave Prague. Proceed against this most powerful human injury that has ever afflicted me with the most powerful means of reaction at my disposal', he postulated dramatically in his diary in 1913, and a century later I eagerly nodded along with all the anxious conviction of somebody who has left her Central European hometown behind too. But now that I am in Prague, I feel cheated. How could Kafka have disparaged it? What was wrong with him?!

I do not have the headspace to resolve this alarming realisation straight away. I am distracted by the fact that, implausibly, somebody named Kafka lives in the building where I am staying. Another unreasonably grand art nouveau façade, and inside a wide, cavernous staircase with tiled floors. At first I shake my head with disbelief every time I pass by the letterbox of this mysterious Kafka. But then I stop by Shakespeare a Synové, or Shakespeare and Sons, Prague's response to Paris's Shakespeare and Company, and get myself an English translation of Bohumil Hrabal's *Inzerát na dům, ve kterém už nechci bydlet*. Even though the title of this short-story collection, published by the iconic Czech humorist in 1965, means 'An Ad for a House Where I No Longer Want to Live', Paul Wilson's English translation was published as *Mr. Kafka and Other Tales*. Ah, here he is again, our friend. The first story in the collection, which Wilson titled 'Mr. Kafka', is called 'Kafkárna' in Czech; I like W. L. Solberg's earlier translation of this title, 'The Kafkorium'. The narrator, one Mr Kafka, wanders around post-war Prague, apparently in search of himself:

'Ma'am,' I say to the old sausage seller, 'did you ever know a Franz Kafka?'

'Oh my Lord!' she says. 'My name is Františka Kafková, and my father, a horsemeat butcher, was František Kafka. Then I knew a headwaiter at the station restaurant in Bydžov who was also called Kafka,' she goes on, leaning closer, her single tooth gleaming in her mouth like a soothsayer's. 'But sir, if you'd like something extra, I can tell you, you're not going to die a natural death' [. . .] and she turns her sizzling sausages with a fork. 'I also read cards,' she goes on.

I feel duly chastised. I am just one obsessive reader of Kafka among many and, in this city patiently suffering under a deluge of such obsessives, many intimate, unique, one-of-a-kind, mysterious, magical, supernatural Kafka connections will obligingly reveal themselves. Almost all fake.

Like the World of Franz Kafka, one of Prague's lowest-rated attractions on TripAdvisor, which occupies an oddly prominent location – Náměstí Franze Kafky 1, just off the Old Town Square, and around the corner from the site of Kafka's birth (the original house has not survived). The World of Franz Kafka, I gather upon perusing its dark, menacing website, is located underground, in a web of medieval corridors and chambers, and promises to transport me inside Kafka's head. It calls itself an 'experience' rather than 'museum' or 'exhibition', and was created by a Czech police photographer and life-long fan of Kafka, so committed to his vision that he ordered the urn with his ashes to be placed in a prominent spot in the World of Franz Kafka upon his death. All of this sounds rather encouragingly wacky to me, and I wonder if perhaps the negative reviews on TripAdvisor were written by some bores who do not appreciate conceptual art. Unfortunately, having descended into the World of Franz Kafka, I can confirm that it is indeed hard to describe it as anything other than a tourist trap. The gloomy crypt is plastered with portentous slogans – 'unmeasurable forces have manipulated our lives since the beginning'; 'precisely these forces are paraphrased within the exhibition following his [Kafka's] example' – paired with generic-looking, grim photographs and videos that do not in fact seem to have anything to do with Kafka.

So if this is fake, what is real? Can Prague offer a sturdy grip on Kafka's world at all? Yes. Yes it does – if you know where to look.

Transformations and Retransformations

As is usually the case, the perfect place to start is Kafka's own work. Here in Prague you read Kafka differently – and I do not mean in the figurative sense, or at least not exclusively. I mean in a very literal sense too. If you want to pick up a copy of one of Kafka's books, whether in German, English, Czech or many other languages, you will easily find one in the numerous souvenir shops and bookstores dotted around Prague's historic centre. But if you look closely, you will discover that the edition you picked up is neither the standard critical edition published by S. Fischer in Germany, nor one of the familiar English editions by Schocken or Penguin. Instead, the volume you are holding in your hands is likely to have been published by a small local press called Vitalis, specialising in the German-language writings of Prague authors in the early twentieth century. Here Kafka is published alongside Gustav Meyrink's *Golem* and Rainer Maria Rilke's *Two Prague Stories*, and Kafka's *Metamorphosis* is accompanied by 'The Retransformation of Gregor Samsa', a short story published in a Prague newspaper just a few months after Kafka's tale of transformation first appeared.

It is a short sequel written by one Karl Brand, a budding author and young tuberculosis sufferer. It begins in the rubbish heap where the insect had been disposed of by the charwoman; it now comes back to life and metamorphoses back into a man. 'The Retransformation of Gregor Samsa' ends on an optimistic note but, just months after the story was published, the twenty-two-year-old author died of tuberculosis, the illness that would eventually kill Kafka too. I find Brand's sequel to *The Metamorphosis* truly poignant: it expresses a hopeless dream of recovery from a deadly disease by writing a new ending to Kafka's story.

I pick up my copy in a tiny tourist bookshop located in a minuscule house – a cottage really – on Zlatá ulička, a row of little dwellings dating back to the sixteenth century squeezed in at the edge of the imposing Prague Castle complex. The name translates as Golden Lane; goldsmiths might have lived here at some point, but probably not the legendary alchemists of its German name Alchimistengasse (Alchemists' Lane). This petite alleyway is one of the top tourist attractions in Prague today and you must pay an entrance fee just to stroll along. I duly pay up because, in a lucky boon for Prague's tourism industry, this is where two of the most famous local myths meet: the mysterious early modern Prague of golems, alchemists and eccentric Habsburg emperors, and the early twentieth-century Prague of Franz Kafka and his strange tales. Kafka's youngest sister Ottla rented the tiny house now occupied by the bookshop in the winter of 1916–17 and let Franz use it for writing on long, cold evenings after work. This is where most of the stories later collected in *A Country Doctor* (1920) were written, Kafka's most substantial collection of stories published during his lifetime. I cannot pass up the opportunity to squeeze myself in here for a little moment, no matter the alarmingly high concentration of other, similarly determined tourists per square metre in the tiny cottage.

But it is not just on Zlatá ulička that you can get yourself a copy of a Vitalis edition of *A Country Doctor* or *The Metamorphosis*: most booksellers and souvenir shops in town seem to stock them. The publisher appears to have a virtual monopoly on Kafka's books in Prague: here, it is difficult to read about Gregor Samsa's transformation without being urged to imagine his retransformation with Brand straight away. Many scholars of Kafka are likely to scoff at this and point out that Brand's little vignette is aesthetically immature and incomparably less complex than *The Metamorphosis*. But I have to confess that I am very partial to my souvenir edition brought back from Prague. I like how it insists on reinscribing Kafka into his local Prague context in very concrete terms, not only reminding us that his texts were being read here decades before Kafka became the global icon he is today, but also capturing the sheer emotional force they wielded over their early readers, just as they continue to do today.

The Vitalis edition of *The Metamorphosis* is not the only souvenir I brought back from Prague. 'I am made of literature, I am nothing else, and cannot be anything else'; ironically, Kafka's comment from 1913 now appears on a mug I bought at the Franz Kafka Museum on the bank of the Vltava River (not to be confused with the World of Franz Kafka near the Old Town Square). In Prague, Kafka lurks behind every corner – as merch: there are tote bags, assorted apparel, fridge magnets, posters. It might be tempting to write it all off as uninteresting, generic tat that could be sold everywhere and nowhere, with Kafka's face easily replaceable by another popular writer, or composer, or contemporary celebrity famous for being famous. And yet the truth is more complicated.

For one thing, if Kafka the writer has become part and parcel of Prague's commodity culture relatively recently, Kafka the family name had already played a similar role during his lifetime. From the youngest age, Kafka's very existence quite literally depended on a lively trade in pretty things: his father ran a store selling 'Galanteriewaren', or fashion accessories, located at one stage in the Old Town Square. The family's name gave rise to the logo featured on the store's business stationery – a jackdaw ('kavka' in Czech) – a piece of trivia significant enough to appear on the first page of Brod's influential early biography of Kafka. Even beyond its actual meaning, the name 'Kafka' simply *sounds* nice – and not just to speakers of European languages. More than a century after the Kafka family first exploited the commercial potential of their name, numerous cafés, stores and businesses across East Asia are named after Kafka, often with no further reference to the Prague author, simply because the name – pronounced 'Kafuka', with an extra vowel to fit Chinese, Japanese and Korean phonologies – sounds unusual but fits the linguistic patterns to pleasing effect, unlike most other European names.

You might think that the brand 'Kafka' has nothing to do with the serious, academic study of his life and work. And yet there is some overlap: his iconic signature – in his distinctive, curving handwriting – features not only on the handle of the Kafka Museum mug but is also written out across the covers of a recent German scholarly edition of Kafka's complete works. Jiří Votruba, the designer of a famous image of Kafka which now adorns most of the themed souvenirs sold in Prague – against a yellow background, a black sketch of a man in a fedora walking down a Prague street with his back to us, the sky above him filled with writing in a made-up language – is no stranger to the scholarly exploration of the subject of his design either, and deeply aware of the tensions inherent in producing it. Asked about his role in merchandising Kafka, Votruba explained:

> I never would have imagined merchandising Kafka before because for me he was a holy figure and this commercial use was against my soul. But my friend persuaded me to try and I made the first design, Franz Kafka walking in the street and the sky is full of literature. It seemed not to be attacking the Kafka spirit, and so this is how it started. And I have to say I know Kafka's life quite well and have read all the books accessible – the last one was the memories of people who knew Kafka personally, like his maid and friends, girlfriends, which was very interesting, and I came to the conclusion that he perhaps would not be so much against it.

As it turns out, Votruba's design was informed by the academic scholarship on Kafka – and the gradual reappearance of Kafka in Prague since the Second World War, culminating in Votruba's iconic design, needs to be understood not as a story of ahistorical commodification, but rather as a process closely connected to the deep historical transformations in this part of Europe.

'Grant Him a Permanent Visa!'

The first plaque in Prague commemorating Kafka, which can still be seen today around the corner from the World of Franz Kafka, was erected in 1965, tracking a change in the official Communist discourse on his work. Communist authorities initially dismissed Kafka as, in the words of Iakov Elsberg, an influential Soviet critic from the 1950s, a 'bourgeois fashion which will pass'. As scholar Veronika Tuckerova explains, Kafka's books were largely unavailable in Czechoslovakia from 1948 to 1957, and then again from 1968 to 1989, although there were exceptions – notably, they circulated continuously in underground samizdat publishing. The ten-year interruption to the official ban on Kafka was brought about by the Khrushchev Thaw after Stalin's death in 1953: Kafka's books could now be published and adapted for the theatre, and the author himself publicly discussed and even commemorated with a plaque marking the location of his birth. No wonder that the very same year – 1965 – saw the publication of Hrabal's story filled to the brim with so many Kafkas.

The event most strongly associated with the rediscovery of Kafka in Communist Czechoslovakia had taken place two years previously, on the eightieth anniversary of his birth. It was an academic conference, but if academic conferences had been formally ranked for 'societal impact' at the time, as they are wont to be today, this one would have been off the charts. The goal of the conference, which took place in Liblice, a castle to the north of Prague, was to see whether Kafka could be reinterpreted to make him more palatable to the Communist authorities. This small-scale testing of the limits of ideological control has often been credited with contributing to the outbreak of the Prague Spring five years later.

The year before the Liblice conference, in 1962, Jean-Paul Sartre – whose infamous fascination with the Soviet Union was now far more critical than it had been immediately after the Second World War, though he still saw himself as a cultural mediator between the two sides of the Iron Curtain – had asked rhetorically in a speech at the Peace Congress in Moscow: 'Who does Kafka belong to, to you or to us; that is, who does understand him better?' and pleaded for Kafka to be 'demilitarised'. Ernst Fischer, one of the speakers at the Liblice conference, similarly pleaded: 'Bring back Kafka's work from its involuntary exile! Grant him a permanent visa!' A number of presenters attempted to make Kafka acceptable to the Communist state apparatus by explicitly opposing the 'capitalist' interpretation of Kafka as a prophet of Communist totalitarianism, and instead framing him as a modernist who at least recognised the problems of capitalism, even if he failed to appreciate, let alone propagate, socialist solutions to these problems. Kafka evocatively depicted alienation under capitalism, the argument went, but did not commit to the socialist alternative, and instead wallowed in bourgeois defeatism. This was a classic move: Thomas Mann's *The Magic Mountain* was cautiously praised in Soviet Russia as a novel that succeeded at exposing capitalist greed but was simultaneously seen as deeply suspicious because it seemed to glorify a passive enjoyment of the excesses of luxury.

The precise significance of the Liblice conference has been disputed. While it has been touted by some as a symbol of cultural de-Stalinisation in Eastern Europe, Tuckerova suggests that in fact it might have been more important to Western, or specifically Western German observers, themselves deeply invested in Kafka's oeuvre, than to the self-understanding of the Czechs. But it would be a mistake to write off the conference as an insignificant, empty gesture by the Communist authorities. Having analysed previously unstudied archival documents, Tuckerova was able to reveal the extent to which the censorship office and even the Central Committee of the Communist Party sought to exert control over the planning, execution and aftermath of the conference. Even the Czechoslovak president at the time, Antonín Novotný, would later go on to reflect on it in his memoirs: 'The Kafka conference had a great impact on our economy . . . anti-Marxist opinions started to spread like a snowstorm, and under their influence industrial development and socialist accumulation decreased, and the party and state discipline weakened.' Novotný's words read like a perverse advertisement for the value of literary scholarship – a force to be reckoned with, since it can apparently wreck a country's economy.

On one level, Novotný's reasoning is ridiculous, of course: in Tuckerova's words, 'This is a typical example of the bizarre ideological discourse with preposterous assumptions and non-sequitur conclusions, characteristic of Communist propaganda, which was looking for any paranoid excuse to explain away the ever-present shortcomings of the command economy.' But on another level, the capability of Kafka's work to penetrate all the way into the heart of Communist bureaucracy is simply stunning, not least because the texts themselves so often cut to the core of the bewilderingly senseless intricacy of bureaucratic processes, which he observed up close in his job at the Workers' Accident Insurance Institute for the Kingdom of Bohemia by day and transposed into intricate literary scenarios by night.

Kafka took up this civil-servant job in the very last years of the existence of the Habsburg Empire with its famously complex administrative and legal structures. In essence, he was a bureaucrat – even though, specialising in the field of industrial accident prevention, he was committed to the needs of individual workers and not just the correctness of formal procedures. While he did spend a lot of his time at a desk, corresponding to the etymological meaning of 'bureaucracy' as 'government by people at desks', he also took many business trips to inspect the provisions for workers in various workplaces, such as factories or quarries, and construct legal cases for improving working conditions. Not only was this mission noble, Kafka's colleagues and superiors also perceived him as a capable and diligent employee. And yet in his letters and diaries Kafka invariably framed his professional occupation as infinitely less fulfilling and valuable than his writing, which often featured interminable, illogical, arbitrary bureaucratic processes doggedly pursued by unhelpful, small-minded, petty officials. Kafka's writing not only captures the ruthless senselessness of many forms of modern bureaucracy, recognisable in various political systems, especially totalitarian ones: it also channels a furtive fascination with such inhumanely intricate structures.

Kafka Returns

As we have seen, the fact that the plaque commemorating Kafka's birth was mounted in 1965 rather than any other year was in no way accidental. It is no accident either that the iconic graphic design by Votruba dates back specifically to 1990, even though he had already been reading Kafka during the Prague Spring of 1968. In the aftermath of the Velvet Revolution in 1989 – during which Votruba designed posters for the Civic Forum, the political formation that succeeded in challenging the Communist regime – three factors made the Kafka design possible: Kafka's works could be openly published in Czech again, public memory narratives were being gradually updated to reflect Prague's multicultural past, and the tide of economic reforms caused small private companies to sprout up all around the former Eastern Bloc. With its kooky English name, Fun Explosive, the company that commissioned Votruba's design, is representative of this wave of new private businesses. So was the company's interest in Kafka, now also fully sanctioned by the highest political authority in the newly democratic country, Václav Havel: one of the most prominent dissident writers of the Communist era, the founder and chairman of the Civic Forum for which Votruba designed posters in 1989, now the country's first democratically elected president since the pre-Communist era, an office he would continue to hold until 2003.

In 1990, just four months into his presidency, Havel gave a short but highly idiosyncratic speech at the Hebrew University of Jerusalem, where he was awarded an honorary degree. He framed the entire speech as 'a brief comment on the subject of Franz Kafka and my presidency'. What is the connection between the two? Havel 'would not be in the least surprised', he said, 'if, in the very middle of being president, [he] were to be summoned and led off to stand trial before some shadowy tribunal.' This seems to have been a generational experience for many a Czech intellectual; Tuckerova detected similar tropes in memoirs and letters of several Czech readers of Kafka who spoke of the trials mounted against them during the Stalinist era in terms directly borrowed from Kafka's *Trial*.

But Havel had always, he said, felt a *special* connection to Kafka and his world:

I'm not an expert on Kafka, and I'm not eager to read the secondary literature on him. I can't even say that I've read everything Kafka has written. I do, however, have a rather special reason for my indifference to Kafka studies: I sometimes feel that I'm the only one who really understands Kafka, and that no one else has any business trying to make his work more accessible to me. And my somewhat desultory attitude to studying his works comes from my vague feeling that I don't need to read and reread everything Kafka has written because I already know what's there. I'm even secretly persuaded that if Kafka did not exist, and if I were a better writer than I am, I could have written his works myself. What I've just said may sound odd, but I'm sure you understand what I mean. All I'm really saying is that in Kafka I have found a portion of my own experience of the world, of myself, and of my way of being in the world.

Admittedly, some of this may sound suspiciously like the deeply unconvincing self-stylisation of the World of

Franz Kafka: no need to read any Kafka, what counts is my vision! But Havel's testimony is both more specific and more self-deprecating, and consequently I find it deeply moving. He goes on to compare himself not only to Kafka, but also his famous protagonists from *The Trial* and *The Castle*, although 'I admit that superficially I may appear to be the precise opposite of all those K.'s – Josef K., the surveyor K., and Franz K.' – but still, he claims with much conviction, 'I feel as though I am constantly lagging behind powerful, self-confident men whom I can never overtake, let alone emulate.' Really, one of the most influential men in Europe at the time feels this way?! Havel is a step ahead of me: 'You may well ask how someone who thinks of himself this way can be the president of a country.' But it is true, he insists: 'The lower I am, the more proper my place seems; and the higher I am, the stronger my suspicion is that there has been some mistake.' This sentiment does indeed come across in Kafka's works time and again, both his fiction and his personal writings. But what felt utterly crushing to Kafka, Havel elevates to the status of a political ethics: 'Every step of the way, I feel what a great advantage it is for me as president to know that I can at any moment, and justifiably, be removed from the position.' To paraphrase Kafka's own words about reading Strindberg, Havel is not reading Kafka to read Kafka, but to lie at his chest. Kafka becomes, if not quite his moral guide, then a source of identification, resonance and comfort.

In twenty-first-century Prague, new memorials to Kafka keep appearing: his legacy is still very much alive, continually shaped and reshaped for new generations of readers. Kafka's complete works were first published in Czech in 2007; the

Franz Kafka Museum opened in 2005. In 2003, on the 120th anniversary of Kafka's birth, a new statue by Jaroslav Róna was installed in what used to be the city's Jewish Quarter, placed between the Church of the Holy Spirit and the Spanish Synagogue, on a square right by one of the many apartments Kafka lived in for a time. The bronze sculpture depicts a small Kafka riding on the shoulders of a large figure in a suit, which, upon closer inspection, turns out to be a free-standing suit empty of a body. It alludes to the tradition of representing 'great men' astride horses on public monuments, but with a 'Kafkaesque' twist – this unusual 'horse' seems to be in the process of dissolving into thin air, a scenario reminiscent of Kafka's 'Wish to Become a Red Indian'. It also alludes to a very specific image from Kafka's 'Description of a Struggle', an early story with an unusually explicit setting in Prague. Or at least it begins in Prague – Charles Bridge makes an appearance – but then the narrator finds himself on a country road in 'a vast but as yet unfinished landscape', seemingly unfurling word by word as the story progresses:

> And now – with a flourish, as though it were not the first time – I leapt onto the shoulders of my acquaintance, and by digging my fists into his back I urged him into a trot. But since he stumped forward rather reluctantly and sometimes even stopped, I kicked him in the belly several times with my boots, to make him more lively. It worked and we came fast enough into the interior of a vast but as yet unfinished landscape.

In a speech celebrating the unveiling of the statue, the sculptor emphasised that the installation of such a monument became possible only now that the country was a democratic republic. Like Votruba, Róna was somebody deeply interested in Kafka's life and work: in 1994, he was the set designer for a Czech film adaptation of one of his novels. In his speech, he compared Kafka's 'prophetic image of the world' to 'a huge iceberg with the biggest part hidden under the water', which 'we can only observe . . . from one point of view'. In a later interview, Róna revealed that he enjoyed returning to the little square to discreetly observe visitors' reactions to the sculpture. Some do not know much about Kafka at all and are confused by the statue, which does not conform to expectations about commemorative monuments: which of the two figures is this Kafka even – surely not the smaller one? Perhaps this confusion might prompt some to learn more about the writer, unlike more traditional monuments of 'great men' we tend to pass on the streets of Europe's capitals without a second thought.

When I first set off for Prague, I was plagued by doubt: would I find much of Kafka here at all? Is the city not a bit of a red herring, so obviously connected to Kafka and yet so utterly changed since his time? All I had read about Kafka's presence in today's Prague had sounded distinctly unappealing: tourist traps, cheap tat in souvenir shops, no original manuscripts or other exhibits in the Franz Kafka Museum, tacky monuments, and little trace of the multicultural Central European past. And yet closely examining the objects and places routinely ignored or disparaged by others has proven richly rewarding. Monuments always tell a story, even if not exactly the one you might have hoped for.

In the last chapter, I traced the international competition over Kafka's legacy, revealed through the placement of German and Austrian plaques on a house he briefly occupied in Berlin, and resulting in a confusing tangle of languages and national affiliations on the oldest and newest monuments to Kafka in Prague: his resting place in the New Jewish Cemetery and 'Franz Kafka's Head' outside a twenty-first-century shopping mall. We can now add further examples to this list. The plaque of 1965 marks a key moment both in Kafka's afterlife in Prague and the story of Communism in Central and Eastern Europe. The graphic design of 1990 reflects a time of transition, when Kafka could officially return to Prague, riding the wave of capitalist reforms, under the auspices of no less a personage than the first democratically elected president of the country. And a curious sculpture from 2003 returns all the way to one of Kafka's earliest stories and introduces a strange twist on the familiar image of a horse rider, a figure which, as we have already seen in Chapter Two, would continue to loom large in Kafka's imagination for years.

From Café Louvre to Café Slavia

Many readers who cultivate a serious interest in Kafka's life and work are dissatisfied with what they see as a touristic commodification of Kafka in today's Prague. Tuckerova, for example, echoes an earlier scholar's complaint that 'the Czechs have not read or understood Kafka', points out that he has not become part of the Czech literary canon, and claims that in contemporary Prague, Kafka 'remains peculiarly absent . . . relegated to the status of a tourist attraction'. This approach strikes me as somewhat misguided: it seems to me that it is not accurate – or productive

– to draw such a stark distinction between earnest reading and mere tourism. As we have seen, Kafka's touristic commodification can also be seen as a peculiar continuation of the family brand from Kafka's lifetime: accessories branded 'Kafka' had been sold in Prague's Old Town already when he was a boy. Kafka himself enjoyed travelling in the footsteps of his favourite writers too – Goethe in Weimar, Flaubert in Paris – and certainly would not have been above getting a Flaubert-themed souvenir or two, preferably 'on the cheap', which was the title of the series of guidebooks he enjoyed thinking up with Brod on their travels.

It is equally useful to remember that the Kafka-themed souvenirs and monuments in Prague in fact reflect the tumultuous history of the region in the twentieth century. To dismiss them is to dismiss the historical specificity of Central Europe. It is not the case that Prague fails to appropriately commemorate Kafka: what foreign visitors may easily miss is that, in a country where cultural continuity has been violently disrupted so many times in the course of the twentieth century, acts of reviving the memory of Kafka will necessarily take a different form to the kind of reverent interest in canonical authors familiar from other European capitals. What might count as a tatty souvenir in Paris or London in Prague emerges as a symbol of peaceful political transformation.

Besides, those who complain that the 'authentic' spirit of Kafka is not much in evidence in today's Prague downplay one key factor. Much of the architecture of Kafka's Prague has survived to this day. In some cases, it is just the magnificent art nouveau and art deco façades that have survived. In other cases, the interiors are original too, sometimes down to the furniture and details of the décor. These sights can be taken in on one leisurely stroll across the city centre. Nice for the tourist, but less so for the man himself: it is a powerful reminder of why Kafka found the city so crammed and oppressive. An acquaintance reminisced years after his death that they once looked down at the Old Town Square out of the window of Kafka's room together. Kafka pointed in the direction of his school, then the university he had attended, finally his office, and commented: 'My whole life is enclosed within this small circle.' Whether or not this poignant memory is accurate, Kafka did indeed spend most of his days within a circle of a little over one mile in diameter.

During my fortnight in Prague, I could have stayed at the outer edge of that circle, in the Franz Kafka Suite in a hotel located in what was Kafka's workplace for fourteen years – that is, almost his entire working life: the Workers' Accident Insurance Institute for the Kingdom of Bohemia. Kafka started working there as a civil servant after just under a year as a clerk at the Prague chapter of Assicurazioni Generali, a private insurance company founded nearly 200 years ago and still in operation. Its Corporate Heritage & Historical Archive still proudly displays Kafka's job application and CV from 1907. At the Workers' Accident Insurance Institute, Kafka worked among a staff which was made up almost entirely of Christian Czechs, but he was well liked: competent, respectful, fluent in Czech and a good writer (of course!), he was promoted several times, making it all the way to the post of senior secretary a few months before his early retirement on medical grounds in 1922, two years before his death. In the last few years before his eventual retirement, as Kafka's health was deteriorating, he was often on leave; still, his surviving office writings – legal reports, case studies, policy proposals – add up to a hefty volume of over 1,000 pages. They were published in German in 2004; a selection is also available in English. These are the things, then, that Kafka had to spend the lion's share of his waking hours writing, when all he wanted to really write was literature. He complained a lot about this job and dreamed of becoming a full-time writer if he only had the financial means to do so. Some of this complaining was done in letters and notes to friends that he wrote on office paper during working hours: an early twentieth-century equivalent to surreptitious texting at your office desk.

Staying at the Franz Kafka Suite seemed initially tempting – the hotel's art nouveau façade dating back to Kafka's times has been lovingly restored, the visitor is greeted by a giant bust of Kafka at the door, and the hotel claims that the suite is located exactly where Kafka's office used to be. But the building's interior has been completely remodelled – and, after all, Kafka was rather miserable here. A writer from Belfast has reported the initial excitement of using his frequent traveller loyalty points to check in at the Franz Kafka Suite some years ago and leave behind a copy of his own novel. He did also try to write another piece while there – but to no avail. I settle for my own mysterious Kafka in an apartment on the other side of the city centre.

I do, however, spend a few days reading innumerable essays by budding writers and other Kafka aficionados who had come to Prague and Berlin in search of Kafka before me. Americans seem particularly well represented in this micro-genre. One essay describes in much detail how its author attempted to track down the hotel Kafka regularly stayed in when visiting Berlin. She is shown a desk and chair that ostensibly stood in Kafka's usual room, invited to sit down on 'his' chair even, but a few years later, she learns more about the history of the hotel and realises the furniture must have been fake. How greedy we all are, the international tribe of Kafka devotees: we each want to have a piece of him just to ourselves. A hairbrush, a chair, a name on a mailbox. Even if he did not manage to decisively determine the interpretation of Kafka's works, Brod succeeded on at least one count: he made a modern saint out of his best friend.

If not the World of Franz Kafka, the Franz Kafka Museum, or Franz Kafka Suite, what might an alternative Kafka itinerary in Prague entail? One of the most enjoyable ways to follow in his footsteps is to visit two different cafés on Národní, in Kafka's time known as Ferdinandova třída (Ferdinand Avenue), named after Emperor Ferdinand I of Austria, before being renamed as Národní třída (National Avenue) in 1919 in celebration of Czechoslovak independence. The interior of the first of these cafés has been preserved, in fact almost unchanged since the first decades of the twentieth century; the second has been restored to its art deco design from the 1920s. I start with Café Louvre, which Kafka was in a habit of frequenting with his friends. Large, spacious, filled with light, it still has its own branded stationery on every table: little notecards and tiny pencils. Unusually, it is located on the first floor, not the ground floor, which means you can look at the little bobbing heads of passers-by from above. There are old-fashioned cakes and rich, thick hot chocolate in small cups. Waiters wear starched aprons, and most of the guests seem local. I spend many a happy hour here during my stay in Prague, leisurely reading

Kafka and jotting down some notes on the tiny notecards. I am used to cramped Oxford cafés, filled to the brim with students and academics jostling for space, usually badly lit and filled with mismatched, rickety tables. While they do have their charm, I would go back to the elegant, spacious Café Louvre in a heartbeat.

Unless given a choice to return to Café Slavia instead: then I would have to think long and hard. A short walk up the street from art nouveau Café Louvre, in Kafka's time art deco Café Slavia – as the name implies – attracted, above all, Czechs. It is located directly opposite the National Theatre with its fabulous deep sky-blue roof twinkling with golden stars. From its huge windows, you can either look at the theatre, or the nearby bridge, which, like the avenue that leads to it, underwent a patriotic name change in 1919 – from Emperor Franz II Bridge to Legion Bridge, after the Czechoslovak Legion that fought in the First World War. Beyond the bridge, there is a breathtaking view of the Vltava River and the mighty Prague Castle.

According to a historical sketch on the café's website, Kafka visited it too; I have not been able to verify this information, but we do know that he saw several Czech plays at the National Theatre. As we have already established, he was not easily put off by nationalistic divisions between local communities and might have popped into Café Slavia before or after one of those plays. Like others in his circles, he saw cafés as an essential ingredient of modern sociability. Oskar Baum, one of Kafka's closest friends from Prague, even jotted down a little sketch relayed to him by Kafka:

A man wants to create the opportunity for groups of

people to come together without being invited. People see and talk to and observe one another without knowing one another. It is a banquet that anyone can define according to his taste, his individual preferences, without imposing on anyone. One can appear and disappear again when one likes, is under no obligation to a host, yet is always welcome, without hypocrisy. When the man is finally able to make this whimsical idea a reality, the reader realises that this experiment at redeeming people from solitude merely – produced the inventor of the first coffeehouse.

The Breakthrough and the Bridge

I come back to Café Slavia several times during my stay in Prague. To get there from the apartment on the north shore of the Vltava River where I am staying, I need to cross one of Prague's many picturesque bridges: the Čech Bridge. That bridge, completed in 1908, was a landmark that Kafka could see from his bedroom window in the top-floor, riverside apartment his family occupied between 1907 and 1913. These were key years in Kafka's life: he finished his law degree and embarked on his professional career, first at Assicurazioni Generali and then at the Workers' Accident Insurance Institute. That riverside apartment is also where Kafka's self-professed literary breakthrough took place one feverish night in the autumn of 1912: the writing of what is to this day one of his most famous stories, *The Judgement*.

It is worth lingering over *The Judgement* for several reasons. At around ten pages, it is a quick read, but the complexity and unexpected strangeness of Kafka's vision are in full evidence here. The events of the story, which is dedicated to Felice Bauer – 'for Fräulein Felice B.', Kafka wrote underneath the title – were indirectly inspired by his life; its deeply meaningful geography corresponds closely to the precise place in Prague where Kafka lived at the time. The story is also directly followed in his notebook by a diary entry that describes both the writing process and the emotions it stirred up in the author in detail, and identifies this event as an unmistakeable breakthrough in Kafka's life as a writer:

This story 'The Judgement' I wrote at one stretch on the night of the 22 to 23 from 10 o'clock in the evening until 6 o'clock in the morning. My legs had grown so stiff from sitting that I could hardly pull them out from under the desk. The terrible strain and joy, how the story unfolded itself before me how I moved forward in an expanse of water. Several times last night I bore my weight on my back. How everything can be risked, how for all, for the strangest ideas a great fire is prepared, in which they die away and rise again. How it turned blue outside the window. Two men walked across the bridge. At 2 o'clock I looked for the last time at the clock. As the maid walked through the hall for the first time, I wrote down the last sentence. Putting out the lamp and daylight. The slight heart pains. The tiredness passing away in the middle of the night. The trembling entrance into my sisters' room. Reading aloud. Beforehand stretching in front of the maid and saying: 'I've been writing until now.' The appearance of the untouched bed, as if it had just been carried in. The confirmed conviction that with my novel writing I am in disgraceful lowlands of writing. Only in this way can writing be done, only with such cohesion, with such complete opening of the body and the soul. Morning in bed. The always clear eyes.

The circumstances of Kafka's creative spurt described here bear an interesting relationship to the events described in *The Judgement* itself. Kafka wrote the story in a single autumn night in 1912; the story takes place on a single spring morning. It opens with the protagonist Georg Bendemann at his desk, having just finished a letter to a friend, now looking out the window at a river with a bridge over it, with green hills in sight on the other shore. This is a precise description of the view out of the apartment in which the Kafkas lived at the time. It is as though Kafka picked up the pen at his desk exactly where Bendemann put it down at his.

The first few paragraphs of the story are taken up with Georg's deliberations about his friend's situation. It is an old friend who moved abroad a long time ago, to Russia, St Petersburg to be exact, where – like Georg – he works as a merchant. But he has not been doing well, his business is floundering, he is lonely. Could one help him in some way? Would he perhaps do better back home? Would he not be offended by an offer of help though, would such an offer not amount to a tacit suggestion that his efforts to establish a life for himself have failed, which would cause the friend much embarrassment? And would his lot improve at all were he to return? Georg does not reach any firm conclusions: it is all very unpleasant, it is difficult to know what to write to his friend, and whether one can even update him on one's own life any more, especially given how *well* one has been doing oneself recently . . . Here the story pivots from Georg considering his friend's situation to an examination of his own circumstances.

Much has changed for Georg in the last couple of years. After the death of his mother, he was left alone with his father, and their relationship has changed. Georg's father has pulled back; Georg has become more decisive, both in his professional and personal affairs. The family business has doubled its number of employees; the sales have quintupled! This, by the by, happens to dwarf the turnover produced by the friend's business in St Petersburg. In his internal monologue, Georg appears at pains not to sound smug, but perhaps is not as successful in this particular endeavour as he is in his *super-hyper booming business* . . . And in his personal life to boot. It would really be too much to mention this to his poor friend, Georg reasons, but as it happens he has just become engaged to one Miss Frieda Brandenfeld, 'a girl from a well-to-do family'. Georg has often spoken to Frieda about this friend, expressed reluctance to invite him to the wedding, to even mention the engagement; why stoke his inevitable resentment at Georg's happiness. But Frieda is unhappy about this foot-dragging, and so on this very spring morning Georg has found himself ending his letter by both reporting on the engagement, and extending a wedding invitation to his friend. Letter in hand, Georg now walks over to his father's bedroom, and this is where the story takes another decisive turn.

Father and Son

Such an encounter in the father's intimate quarters is unusual, we learn: in their daily life, the two men interact almost exclusively at work. In his bedroom, the father initially comes across as frail and vulnerable. The room is dark and fuggy, there is uneaten food on the table; the father is not dressed for the day, his eyesight is weak. And yet when he gets up to greet his son, Georg's impression of his father momentarily changes: 'His heavy dressing-gown opened as he walked, the skirts flapping round him – "My father is still a giant," Georg said to himself.' This cognitive dissonance – is the father a feeble old man or a mighty giant? – will last for quite a while.

Georg informs his father that he decided to write to the friend in St Petersburg about his engagement after all. '"Yes, to your friend," said his father with emphasis.' Now what is he implying here? As the conversation continues, we gradually find out. The father claims that since his mother's death, Georg has been acting suspiciously, misleading his father in various matters. 'But because we are discussing this matter in particular, this letter, I beg you, Georg, do not deceive me. It's a little thing, it's not worth the breath it takes to say it, so don't deceive me. Do you really have this friend in St Petersburg?' Georg's response is evasive, but perhaps he is just trying to shield his ailing father, who might be confused: 'Let's leave my friend be. A thousand friends wouldn't replace my father. Do you know what I believe? You're not looking after yourself enough.' He goes on about his concerns for his father's health for a while. But the father persists. He plainly states what the reader will have been suspecting for some time: 'You have no friend in St Petersburg.'

Georg gently helps his father to his armchair and tries to remind him of the friend and his situation. Might Georg be telling the truth? Is the father simply senile and thus forgetful? Georg notices more worrying signs – the father is toothless, his hair is unkempt, his underwear not particularly clean – and berates himself silently for his neglect. The father will have to move in with him and his bride in order to be properly taken care of, he resolves. Georg carries his father to bed, and the father is anxious to be covered. 'Am I well covered over now?' he asks twice, with urgency. But Georg's response – 'Quietly, now. You are well covered over' – all of a sudden unleashes something truly horrible. The father now clearly comes across as a mighty giant rather than a feeble old man, so huge that he can touch the ceiling – although the fact that he must steady himself like this lest he fall off the bed on which he is standing brings out the absurdity of the proceedings:

'No!' shouted the father [. . .] he threw the bedspread back with such strength that for a moment it opened out completely in its flight, and stood upright in his bed. With only one hand he held lightly onto the ceiling. 'You wanted to cover me over, I know, my little sprig, but I'm not covered over yet. And even if this is the last of my strength, it's enough for you, too much for you. Of course I know your friend. He would have been a son after my own heart. That is why all these years you have been deceiving him too. Why else?' Georg looked up at the nightmare image of his father. The friend in St Petersburg, whom the father now suddenly knew so well, moved him as never before. He saw him lost in far-off Russia. He saw him at the door of an empty, plundered shop. Among the wrecked shelves, the shattered stock, the broken gas brackets, he was just about still standing. Why did he have to go away so far!

One word is particularly important here. The German 'zudecken' has similar connotations to the English 'cover over' or 'cover up': it is initially used to describe a physical action of covering the father with a blanket, but then morphs into an accusation of a misdeed, of attempting to covertly push the father aside.

At the same time, the faraway friend suddenly comes back into focus again. The word 'Fremde', which means 'a foreign, unfamiliar place', and related words are used several times in the story – the friend seems very far removed from home, but also clearly functions as a prism through which everything at home is being refracted. The father does not deny his existence any more, but declares himself the friend's 'representative here on the spot'. Suddenly the friend from St Petersburg appears as an avatar of both protagonists of the story, both Georg and his father – or perhaps a symbol of their power struggle, since the father suddenly announces:

'How you amused me today when you came and asked whether you should write to your friend about your engagement. He knows all about it already, you young fool! He knows all about it already! I wrote to him because you forgot to take my writing things away from me. That's why he hasn't come for years. He knows everything a hundred times better than you do yourself.

He crumples up your letters in his left hand, while in his right he holds up my letters to read!'

The story began with Georg's letter to his friend: but now, with the story almost at its end, the letters multiply, and writing utensils turn into veritable weapons. The friend in St Petersburg emerges as the fulcrum of the father–son conflict by deciding whose letters to read and whose letters to destroy – and, by extension, whose version of events to believe. At this point in the story, the authority is firmly with the father, and it culminates in his unexpected pronounce-ment, or titular 'judgement', to Georg: 'I condemn you now to death by drowning!' Note that the German verb used here is 'verurteilen'; just like in English, the German word 'Urteil' can mean both a judgement in a judiciary context and a more general, everyday judgement – an interpretation. It is as though by gaining the upper hand in the contest of inter-pretations the father also gains the power to sentence Georg to death like an omnipotent court.

Georg not only accepts this strange sentence, but also reverts to the role of a child. No trace of a successful, inde-pendent, commanding businessman is left. He runs out of the house and on to the bridge which he looked at in the opening sentences of the story; his last words are '"Dear parents, I did always love you"', before 'he let[s] himself drop'. Georg throws himself into the river; we presume he drowns. But we know that Kafka, who clearly identi-fied himself with Georg to some extent, was a very good swimmer; in fact his favourite civilian swimming school was right next to the real-life bridge that inspired the bridge in the story. Even more suggestively, the diary entry that directly follows the manuscript of *The Judgement* in Kafka's note-book compares the 'unfolding' of the story before the writer to the process of 'moving forward in an expanse of water' – that is, to swimming. The strange judgement pronounced by Georg's father might condemn him to drown, but then Georg's drowning engenders Kafka's creativity; it allows him to swim in the ocean – or rather, river – of creativity.

The last sentence of the story reads: 'At this moment there flowed over the bridge an absolutely unending stream of traffic.' Much ink has been spilled teasing out the connotations of the word 'Verkehr', which can mean traffic, but also intercourse. But here it chimes in with the image of swimming too, further emphasised by the word 'stream' added by the English translator: Kafka unblocks and revels in an unending traffic of ideas which, he feels, finally flows freely.

Another Son, Another Father

Kafka's own relationship with his father was famously fraught. Hermann Kafka grew up in poverty in a small Czech village. His marriage to middle-class Julie Löwy, move to Prague, and eventually the founding of the family retail business in the very centre of the city all constituted personal and professional triumphs. As the eldest child and the couple's only son to survive infancy – by the time Franz turned five, his two younger brothers had died of childhood illnesses, at the ages of six months and fifteen months – he was expected to carry the momentum of the family's social ascent. But Franz was uninterested in the family business and, despite his prestigious law degree and an attractive new job as a civil servant in the field of accident insurance, by 1912 – when he wrote *The Judgement* – he had found neither personal fulfilment nor, he felt, his father's acceptance. Hermann did not understand or approve of his son's literary ambitions and their attendant emotional torment.

By all accounts, Kafka's father was brawny, coarse and domineering. Most of these accounts, of course, stem from the son himself. In 1919, he penned one of the most extraordinary documents of his life: a long letter to his father, in which he employs all his literary and rhetorical talent to cast light on their difficult relationship. It is truly a great piece of writing: energetic, precise, fully formed, written all the way through – unlike so much of Kafka's literary writing, there are no loose ends or unfinished sentences here. 'Dearest Father,' it begins, 'you asked me recently why I maintain that I am afraid of you. As usual, I was unable to think of any answer to your question, partly for the very reason that I am afraid of you, and partly because an explanation of the grounds for this fear would mean going into far more details than I could even approximately keep in mind while talking.' What follows resembles one of those imaginary rants one composes in her head in response to some particularly enraging encounter or exchange, hours after the fact: one where your logic is devastatingly unassailable but at the same time you manage to sound entirely rational, reasonable, courteous even.

In the letter, Franz details particularly telling childhood memories; describes how he has always felt weak and frail alongside his father's overbearing physicality; blow by blow, goes through his father's role in various formative experiences of his adult years – failed engagements, professional milestones and finally his writing. Whenever a piece of his was published and came in the post, his father would not have a look, would not even stop his card game, but just say – in what we surmise must have been a dismissive tone – to 'put it on the bedside table', presumably never to be read. And yet 'the aversion you naturally and immediately took to my writing was, for once, welcome to me', Franz claims, 'because to me that formula' – 'put it on my bedside table' – 'sounded something like: "now you are free!"' Even if this did not constitute any real freedom, he explains, his writing created a unique space for communication with his father in a way that was impossible in real life: 'My writing was all about you; all I did there, after all, was to bemoan what I could not bemoan upon your breast.'

Many readers over the years have taken Kafka's letter to his father as the master key to his whole oeuvre, the smoking gun to prove that the meaning of his strange stories can in fact be determined, that what they ultimately mean is this: Franz felt stifled by Hermann and writing offered an opportunity to rebel, but the rebellion always ended up futile. There are certainly many elements in *The Judgement* that resonate with such an interpretation: the fantasy of a weak, frail father, who turns out to be strong and in control after all; the centrality of the family business; the son's act of writing being eventually revealed as ineffectual, unequal to the father's power. Even the final, mysterious judgement of the father in the story finds an echo in the later letter: 'What was always incomprehensible to me was your total lack of feeling for the suffering and shame you could inflict on me with your words and judgements. It was as though you had no notion of your power.' It is as though the story hyperbolically illustrates the extent of the father's power. Franz might be the writer, but it is Hermann's 'words and judgements' that wield power in the real world.

Still, I do not think such a heavily biographical approach is sufficient, or even the most helpful, as a lens through which to view Kafka's works. Many sons have domineering fathers, but we rarely come to care about other people's family dynamics. We do not care about Kafka's writing because of his biography; we care about his biography because of his writing. And this writing has an astonishing power to resonate with people even if they do not share Kafka's life experiences. I am not a son, and my father is nothing like Georg's father in *The Judgement*, or like Hermann Kafka. And yet I still find *The Judgement* impossible to forget: I chuckle whenever I think of Georg's humble-bragging to his possibly imaginary friend, shudder each time I recall the father's fateful pronouncement – 'I condemn you now to death by drowning!' – and the 'absolutely unending stream of traffic' never fails to hypnotise me when I try to visualise the bridge at the end of the story. Kafka transcended his biography, transmorphed the frustrations of his life into a repertoire of endlessly suggestive images and emotional tensions that far exceed the specifics of his own psychological conflicts and anxieties.

Franz's letter, by the way, never reached his father. According to Brod, Franz gave it to his mother, but she sent it back to her son instead of passing it on to her husband. We do not know the details. As with the epistle in *The Judgement*, the primary function of this real-life missive was not as a possible avenue for communication, but rather as a channel for emotional release and power struggle.

Readers' Judgement

Even if Kafka's father never read *The Judgement*, over the years the story has exercised the imagination of one group of readers in particular: literary theorists of all persuasions. In 2002, a whole volume was put together in Germany using this little story as a convenient case study to introduce ten different schools of literary theory: hermeneutics, structuralism, reception theory, sociology of literature, psychoanalysis, gender studies, discourse analysis, systems theory, intertextuality and deconstruction. As the editors point out, the very title of the story might be used not only to describe the stark judgement pronounced by the father at the end, but also the readers' *own* judgement – their understanding of the events of the story and the relationships between the characters. Once again, as so often with Kafka, the focus shifts from the author to his readers.

When we talk about readers, though, we might have several different things in mind. Sometimes what we mean are 'professional' readers – literary scholars, who produce 'readings', or interpretations, of literary texts according to established disciplinary protocols. But when literary scholars themselves refer to 'readers', they usually have in mind so-called 'implied' or 'ideal' readers. Both these terms are used to denote a 'hypothetical' reader: in literary critic Andrew Bennett's words, the person at 'whom the text is directed' and who can 'get the most out of a particular text' – 'equipped in terms of knowledge, sympathies and prejudices, strategies of reading, previous experience of reading'. But this normative conception of an abstract reader implied by the text can be extremely limiting when one considers its actual, real-life readers.

In my own work, I am particularly interested in the experiences of just such varied, diverse real-life readers across time and space, although it is much more difficult to get a sense of them. After all, 'implied' or 'ideal' readers are creative reconstructions based on a careful reading of a literary text, and professional readers, whom I often refer to as 'academic readers', leave behind books and articles. Meanwhile, others – whom I like to call 'non-academic readers', since other available descriptors, like 'lay', 'amateur' or 'general', strike me as either too vague or loaded with all sorts of unnecessary judgements – do not tend to leave behind any systematic written evidence of their encounters with books. But, as you have seen in this book, there are other ways to learn about how and why people read. Common examples of such sources include journalistic reviews, letters from readers to authors, marginal notes in books and – in our Internet age – posts on social media. Histories of manuscripts, book editions and translations can yield fascinating insights too, and so can cognitive studies, where readers' reactions are analysed in laboratory experiments. We have seen samples of almost all these sources already, and will learn about some specific translations as well as an example of marginalia in Vladimir Nabokov's copy of Kafka's *Metamorphosis*, in the chapters to come.

Nabokov was, of course, a famous writer himself, and writers tend to be among the most vocal and creative readers out there. Other writers' books often serve as explicit or implicit inspiration for their own works, and the same is true of other artists. We have seen plenty of examples of this process already. We have also seen how commemorative plaques, statues and speeches, and even tourist souvenirs can offer us unexpected insights into collective reading practices in a given time and place, for example Communist Prague.

Sometimes all we get are mere glimpses of very specific readers, but even such glimpses can often be fascinating. Thinking back to Kafka's feverish diary note which follows the manuscript of *The Judgement*, we may want to linger on one particular passage: 'The trembling entrance into my sisters' room. Reading aloud.' This tells us exactly who the very first readers, or rather listeners, of this story were: Franz's younger sisters Valerie, known as Valli, and Ottilie, known as Ottla. (The eldest sister Gabriele, known as Elli, married in 1910, so was no longer living with her parents.) Kafka does not tell us how his sisters reacted, perhaps because what he really cared about in the moment was his *own* reaction: the following day, he read out *The Judgement* again to a gathering of friends and it moved him so much that he cried a little – the only detail of the reading that he included in his diary. He felt confirmed in his conviction that the story was 'indubitable'.

To the two groups of people who got to hear *The Judgement* almost as soon as Kafka committed it to paper – his sisters and his friends – we can perhaps add one more person. The passage in Kafka's diary about reading out the story to his sisters is immediately followed by: 'Beforehand stretching in front of the maid and saying: "I've been writing until now."' This reminds us of the presence of at least one other person in the house: the maid. Like most of the women employed in the Kafka household over the years, she was Czech, so even if she had heard the story, she likely would not have understood the German. Kafka's maids gained entry to his literature in a very different way.

In the first sentence of *The Man who Disappeared*, for example, we meet 'the seventeen-year-old Karl Roßmann, who had been sent to America by his poor parents because a servant-girl had seduced him and had a child by him'. This chillingly unsympathetic account positions the maid as the guilty party responsible for Karl's forced emigration, and yet the narrative perspective is so clearly one-sided that it immediately raises the possibility of bias: the question of guilt, responsibility and culpability will remain key to the story.

A maid also makes a brief appearance at the end of *The Judgement*: Georg passes her on the stairs while dashing for the bridge, and she cries out: 'Jesus!' On the surface, this is just a conventional cry of someone startled – but, as with many of Kafka's texts, an undercurrent of messianic sacrifice can be detected in the character of the protagonist condemned to death for an amorphous crime, so the maid's scream can also be seen as a highly significant identification of Georg with Christ. Here again the maid is seemingly relegated to a mere background role and yet might hold a key to the whole story.

The Czech women who worked in the Kafka household shaped his literary imagination in yet another, even more important way too. It is largely from them that Kafka initially learnt Czech, and linguists have suggested that German might not have emerged as his dominant language until he was enrolled in a German-speaking school at the age of six. All around him, Czech and German were vying for primacy. The majority of Prague's population spoke Czech, but most members of the social and economic elite spoke German. This was causing much tension, which would ultimately culminate during and in the immediate aftermath of the

Second World War. Physical manifestations of this tension can still be seen in Prague today. The building that used to be the New German Theatre in Kafka's time – a response to the Czech National Theatre, with busts of Goethe, Schiller and Mozart adorning its neoclassical façade – has housed the Czech State Opera since the Second World War. The German busts were removed after the war, but are now back up. Another cultural centre from Kafka's time, Deutsches Haus – German House – was transformed into Slovanský dům – Slavic House – in 1945. But already, decades earlier, the logo of Kafka's father's store had two distinct versions: the branch on which the jackdaw sits on one morphed from an oak, symbolically associated with Germany, to a less distinctive leafy bough on the other, more suitable for Czech customers.

Tale Without End

The uneasy but fertile coexistence of German and Czech symbols, cultures and languages in Prague is reflected in the opening paragraph of one of my favourite little tales by Kafka, 'The Cares of a Family Man', written in the little house on Zlatá ulička. It introduces the name of a curiously ungraspable creature known as Odradek:

> Some say the word Odradek is Slavonic in origin, and they try on this basis to demonstrate the word's construction. Others are of the opinion that its origin is German, and that it is only influenced by Slavonic. But the uncertainty of both interpretations probably allows us to conclude that neither applies, especially as neither

of them offers any help in discovering the meaning of the word.

As the little story continues, we learn that Odradek cannot be grasped because it – or he, as both pronouns are used in the text – is 'extraordinarily nimble' and always on the move. Even its/his physical form and appearance are difficult to describe:

> It looks at first like a flat, star-shaped spool for thread, and it does in fact appear to be wound round with thread, though it seems as if these are only old, torn scraps of yarn of various kinds and colours knotted into string, but also matted together. But it is not only a spool: a little rod sticks out crosswise from the middle of the star, and another one is fitted into this rod at a right angle.

And so the description goes on. It is an extraordinarily complex text, and there are many reasons why Odradek is so difficult to grasp – both to physically catch, and to intellectually comprehend – but one of these reasons, announced in the very first paragraph, concerns the differences between Germanic and Slavonic languages. The ending '-ek' is a typical Slavonic ending for diminutives: just like in French you can add '-on' to many words to indicate small size or young age – 'chat' means 'cat', 'chaton' means 'kitten' – in Czech, you can accomplish the same by adding the ending '-ek'. The prefix 'od-' in Slavonic languages indicates undoing or countering some process, or movement away from something; the stem 'rad' means 'glad' or 'happy'. So how could we construe the meaning of 'Odradek' based on all this linguistic information? 'Unhappy little creature'? But what about German etymology? 'Rad' means 'wheel', 'Ecke' means 'corner'; both shapes play a role in the odd description of Odradek's physical form. There is also the Czech verb 'odradit', with equivalents in other Slavonic languages, which means 'to dissuade'. Interestingly though, this verb in fact comes from the German noun 'Rat', advice. In a way, such philological musings are a red herring: the story does not lead us towards one correct interpretation of Odradek's name. But in another way, these musings are central to the tale. Odradek is suspended between Slavonic and Germanic etymologies not to the exclusion of one or the other, but necessarily containing multitudes: both are necessary, but neither is sufficient on its own.

The Germanic and the Slavonic meet in the name of one of the most famous Czech writers too: Božena Němcová. Her surname, which she took from her husband, is common in Czech and means 'German', or 'mute' – as in, someone who cannot speak *our* language; most Slavonic languages to this day derive their name for Germany from this etymology, reflecting the difficulties of intercultural contact going back more than a millennium. Scholars have long pointed out the importance of Němcová's writings to the formation of Kafka's literary imagination. Kafka himself explained in one of his first letters to Milena Jesenská, his lover and translator into Czech, that he learnt the 'melody' of the Czech language from Němcová. We know that extracts from her work were included in his school textbooks; that he bought an illustrated edition of her classic novel *Babička* (*The Grandmother*, 1855) to read out to his sisters; that the rural setting of *Babička*, as well as some specific plot details, influenced his own novel set in the countryside, *The Castle*; and that he particularly valued Němcová's letters.

But when I first came across her name in my research on Kafka, a different book immediately sprang to mind. Growing up, I was aware of Němcová as the author of *Národní báchorky a pověsti* (*National Fairy Tales and Legends*, 1845–8). On my bookshelf, the Polish translation of her Czech fairy tales sat next to Charles Perrault from France, the Brothers Grimm from Germany and Hans Christian Andersen from Denmark – which, I now realise, gives away my upbringing in Eastern Europe. I found Němcová's stories magnetic, as unsettling and baffling as only the very best fairy tales are. One tale I returned to so often as a child that as soon as I saw Němcová's name mentioned as an influence on Kafka, something popped open in my brain like a jack-in-the-box. Here is 'Povídka bez konce' – in English, 'A Tale Without End':

> Once upon a time, about sunset, a little shepherd lad was pasturing his sheep, near a wide brook. Of course the boy was in a great hurry to get home, where he knew a good supper was waiting for him. Now the wide brook had only a narrow plank for a bridge, so that the sheep were obliged to cross over, in a line, one at a time. Now children, let us wait till the boy has driven all his sheep over the bridge, then I will finish my story.

But this English translation leaves out the crucial final paragraph which so disturbed and fascinated me as a child:

Listeners are waiting; but when their patience is running out, they encourage more storytelling. Then they are told that there were many sheep, so they have not yet passed. Sometimes later, the children demand a continuation, and then they are told again that the sheep have not yet passed, or that by the time they all passed, it was already morning, so the shepherd did not even drive them home, but grazed them anew.

This is a very pragmatic approach to storytelling: what is the purpose of a tale? To keep children occupied. But some children can never get enough and ask for more, more, more. And so a fatigued parent or nanny comes upon a solution. This tale never ends – there is no conclusion, no resolution, no explanation. It is tempting to imagine Kafka encountering this tale as a child and reacting like I did: with immense frustration, but also fascination with this unsettling mode of storytelling that goes against the grain, evoking our expectations about how narratives begin, progress and end, only to ultimately violate them by withholding narrative progression, instead suspending us in the permanent opening gambit of the tale. And yet clearly some form of momentous development does take place: if not in the text, then in the child reader, whose understanding of what is fair, and possible, in literature – as in life – is turned on its head. Or, to put it in less portentous a tone: the future storyteller learns the power of bamboozling his audience.

This mechanism is, of course, something that Kafka would play with his whole life. The almost mechanical, schematic repetition of Karl's failures and disappointments in *The Man who Disappeared*; the essence of Josef

K.'s fate sketched out already in the opening scene of *The Trial*; the frustrating circularity of *The Castle*. The most similar in structure to 'A Tale Without End' is 'Before the Law', Kafka's famous parable from *The Trial*, published as a standalone piece in his lifetime. In it, a man from the country comes to the Law – what exactly that Law is or entails is never made clear – and asks the doorkeeper for access. 'But the doorkeeper says he cannot grant him entry now. The man considers, and then asks whether this means that he might be allowed entry later. "It is possible", says the doorkeeper, "but not now".' The door is open, but the doorkeeper tells the man that he is powerful, and there are many more doorkeepers, even more powerful, on the way to the Law. The man decides to wait: the doorkeeper gives him a stool. 'There he sits for days and years. He makes many efforts to be let in, and wearies the doorkeeper with his pleading.' The man turns 'childish'; at one point he even begs the fleas on the doorkeeper's fur coat collar for help. But to no avail: finally, as the man lies dying, it occurs to him to ask why nobody beside him has ever come to the door to ask for access to the Law. Here is the doorkeeper's answer, with which the enigmatic tale ends: 'Nobody else could be granted entry [here], for this entrance was meant only for you. I shall go now and close it.'

For all their obvious differences, it seems to me that 'Before the Law' is animated by the same basic impulse that made 'A Tale Without End' so unforgettable to me as a child. Both are set in a rudimentary landscape – countryside, where the only architectural feature of note is a narrow access point from one realm to another, whether a bridge or a series of doors; both are populated by small, sparse casts of characters – shepherd and sheep; man from the country, doorkeeper, and the fleas on his coat. Crucially, both tales are governed by the contrast between 'now' and 'later': in both patience is tested, but not rewarded. Both hinge on an unresolved narrative paradox, and both, at their core, are about power: the power of the doorkeeper over the man from the country, of the Law over its subjects, but also of adults over children, of storytellers over their audiences.

I Came a Long Way to Discover a Poor Substitute for Your Company

Having said all that, I am not aware of any concrete evidence that Kafka knew Němcová's tales – and yet I find this putative connection between the two writers thrilling, which tells me something important about how I operate as a reader. Like many readers, whether in or outside academia, I love uncovering such traces, identifying obscure sources like a detective on a case. With Kafka in particular, the temptation to explain away the strangeness of his writing by pointing out what other text, event, person or place influenced it is always there. On one level, it is ultimately futile. Even if I could prove one day that Kafka had indeed read those tales, the best I could then say is that they might have played a role in shaping 'Before the Law', among many other influences. Even if I managed to locate a long-lost note from the time Kafka was working on this text that would explicitly state: 'thinking of Němcová's *Tale Without End*' – which is not impossible: the diary entry commenting on *The Judgement* records 'thoughts of Freud', alongside three other sources – it would still not really 'solve' the mystery of Kafka's parable. The explanatory power of such investigations remains limited. But on another level, it is not a pointless exercise. This is, after all, how we make sense of the world: by looking for connections, making comparisons, pursuing associations.

Looking for sources that might have influenced our favourite writers is also one way of bridging the chasm of history and culture that separate us. In this case, it is my way of coming closer to Kafka – not unlike travelling to Prague in search of his afterlife. For many, the ultimate moment of connection of this kind can be established through a pilgrimage to the writer's grave. On my last day in Prague I go to visit Kafka's grave too. The weather is bad – it is cold and rainy – and you have to take a long ride on the metro from the city centre to get here: small wonder that the place is almost empty. But following the directions of a large sign by the entrance, I think of people who came here before me.

In 1994, exactly seventy years after his death, Czech-Israeli journalist, translator and Holocaust survivor Ruth Bondy stood at Kafka's grave. In her hand, she held one of the many notes – in Romanian, Italian, French and many other languages besides – left there by Kafka's readers. One was in English: 'I came a long way to discover a poor substitute for your company.' The note captured the intimate voice of an unknown reader speaking to Kafka in a foreign tongue across time and space. It was overheard by another reader, Bondy, who was born in Prague a year before Kafka's death, and yet only discovered his work in Israel after the Second World War. She spent her life in search of the lost world of

Jewish life in Central Europe, of which Kafka is perhaps the most famous symbol.

The note, which Bondy was allowed to keep – it can still be seen in the National Library of Israel in Jerusalem today – might strike you as almost unbearably, pathetically melancholic. Kafka died young; the world he and Bondy grew out of was destroyed soon after; many of his writings were lost in the process; perhaps the cultural knowledge and experience needed to fully understand them were gone forever too. But to me, this note is full of hope and excitement. It captures so well the way that we can be so fiercely invested in literary voices, beyond the boundaries of language, place and time. In the act of lamenting the impossibility of a relationship with Kafka, the English reader paradoxically establishes a strangely poignant connection to him and his world – as well as his other readers: Ruth Bondy, who picked up their note, but now also you and me.

On the cold and rainy day of my own visit to Kafka's grave, I spot a couple of notes too, but the ink is streaking down the paper. And yet I manage to catch a glimpse of a whole host of readers who come here in a different way. A local newspaper reports that according to Chaim Koči, the chairman of the local *chevra kadisha*, or burial society, responsible for the ritual administration of Jewish cemeteries in Prague, tens of thousands of tourists from around the world visit the New Jewish Cemetery each year. But just before the coronavirus pandemic hit, Koči observed a new trend: 'The most numerous groups were tourists from South Korea who came to pay tribute to the memory of Kafka.' This is yet another sign I encounter in my search for Kafka's metamorphoses around the world that Seoul is the place to be. But before I set off for Korea, I want to think more about the role Judaism and Jewishness played in Kafka's life, and the many Jewish readers over the years who – like Bondy – felt a special connection to him.

4

Jerusalem

Jewish Kafka

Jewish Readers' Kafka

At the end of the last chapter, we met a Jewish reader of Kafka who was born in a world recognisably his, but spent most of her life in a very different reality. This is an important point: while there has sometimes been a tendency to speak of Jewish readings or interpretations of Kafka as though they originated from a uniform experience or identity, in fact they grow out of a multitude of points of view and perspectives, interconnected but not the same. Even the earliest of Kafka's Jewish readers, his friends belonging to similar social circles in Prague, were informed by a variety of concerns and commitments: for example, some were deeply religious, while others were not, and some were dedicated to Zionism as a political movement formed in Central Europe in the late nineteenth century and associated especially with Theodor Herzl, whom we briefly met in Chapter 2, while others remained sceptical. For many – including, as we shall see, Kafka himself – such commitments were also flexible and changeable. In other parts of the Austro-Hungarian Empire and the German Empire even more variables came into play, and Jewish communities in Eastern Europe in particular developed forms of worship, politics, linguistic identity, and ways of life that differed from Jewish experiences in Western Europe – something that deserves our closer attention because it particularly interested Kafka.

Jewish readers encountering Kafka's works in the decades since his death have been just as diverse in their experiences and viewpoints. From German Jewish philosophers, like Walter Benjamin and Hannah Arendt, to representatives of the State of Israel, including judges at Israel's Supreme Court, to numerous Israeli citizens and members of the multicultural and multilingual Jewish diaspora, Jewish readers represent a wealth of differing approaches to Kafka's life, work and afterlife. Many different experiences of and approaches to Jewishness played a role during the recent series of trials over the ownership of a portion of Kafka's manuscripts, which, after more than a decade of legal proceedings, ended up arriving in the National Library of Israel in Jerusalem in 2019.

What Benjamin Balint evocatively calls 'Kafka's Last Trial' centred around the question of the rightful place for a number of Kafka's manuscripts. These manuscripts were inherited by Eva Hoffe from her mother, Esther Hoffe, who in turn received them from Brod as his secretary and close friend – possibly also lover. The three primary parties involved were Eva Hoffe, the National Library of Israel and the German Literature Archive in Marbach. The library claimed that the manuscripts should pass into its stewardship, based on its interpretation of Brod's will. Eva Hoffe's position was that the manuscripts were her personal possessions, and she had the right to sell them – for example to the Marbach archive, which had already acquired the manuscript of *The Trial* from her mother in the 1980s. Ultimately, the Israeli Supreme Court ruled in favour of the National Library of Israel, stating that Kafka's manuscripts should be housed there as part of the cultural heritage of the Jewish people.

In a much-discussed essay, pointedly titled 'Who Owns Kafka?', influential Jewish American critic Judith Butler argued that 'the legal case rest[ed] on the presumption that it is the state of Israel that represents the Jewish people' – a presumption Butler did not share. But Balint contends that it was not the case that 'only the Israelis had interests' in the trial, and the German archive represented 'an unobjectionably disinterested, neutral, even passive' perspective. For Balint, 'This reflects a position of strength, of a majority culture: only those who have fulfilled their interests can speak in a "disinterested" way, and only those who have accumulated literary capital can allow themselves the luxury of persuading themselves of pure timeless universality of literature.' The trial functioned as both a practical process of negotiation to settle where a chunk of Kafka's manuscripts would be kept, and a pretext for a more theoretical negotiation of both Kafka's legacy and the self-understanding of various Jewish – and non-Jewish – communities around the world.

The viewpoints and interpretations of many different Jewish readers of Kafka over the course of a whole century contributed to the trial, starting with the earliest reader of them all – Max Brod. While Kafka was still alive and Brod was seeking to boost his friend's career, he famously mounted a far-fetched argument: despite never addressing

Jewishness directly in his literature, Kafka is the most Jewish author of all because his yearning for a sense of belonging in a community – implicitly, a Jewish community – is the greatest. More recently, Dan Miron, a leading scholar of modern Hebrew and Yiddish literature at the Hebrew University of Jerusalem, has written on Kafka's central position within what he calls 'modern Jewish literatures', written in and drawing on various languages, an idea he posits as his preferred alternative to 'the Jewish literary canon', defined more exclusively as literature written in modern Hebrew. Through Kafka, Miron seeks to restore a sense of continuity, breadth and diversity of the Jewish experience and identity as reflected in twentieth-century literature.

Kafka and Zionism

But other readers are not satisfied positioning historical Kafka in the broader landscape of Jewish writing, and instead find imaginative ways of projecting him into the future that he did not experience, but which saw the establishment of the State of Israel. In an unconventional academic article from 2016, to take one example, Iris Bruce, a leading scholar of Kafka's engagement with Jewish – especially Zionist – themes and motifs, invites her readers to imagine what would have happened had Kafka moved to Mandatory Palestine with Dora Diamant in 1924.

In Bruce's alternative history, the pair first work as agricultural labourers on a kibbutz, then as teachers. Kafka begins writing again: he revises *The Man who Disappeared* for publication, except that now Karl Roßmann emigrates to Palestine, not America, and does not disappear, but begins a new life – as a member of a horse patrol (his surname, remember, means 'horse rider') protecting Jewish settlements from Arab attacks. But the end of the novel, under its new title – *Driftwood* – undermines Roßmann's actions, depicting 'both Arabs and Jews as helpless "driftwood", at the mercy of selfish, greedy and power-hungry authority figures at all levels of society'. Outside of the realm of his fiction, Bruce's fictional Kafka supports peaceful efforts to create a state in which both Jews and Arabs can thrive. He also rewrites *The Trial*, which finally comes out in 1958 and becomes his 'seminal work about the Holocaust'; a rewritten version of *The Castle* comes out five years later as a 'Zionist epic', opening with Hitler's speech at the Prague Castle in 1939, which prompts the protagonist to emigrate to Palestine to work as a land surveyor there. His three major novels are included in the 1966 citation for 'Israeli writer' Franz Kafka, who becomes the country's first recipient of the Nobel Prize in Literature, shortly before his death in 1968; he turns into a literary celebrity in his new homeland, and today 'all major Israeli cities have important streets or buildings named after Kafka'. In between Kafka's imaginary Nobel and death lies the 1967 Arab–Israeli War: in Bruce's version, his life becomes inextricably interwoven with the history and politics of the Middle East.

In another article, Bruce argued that Kafka 'has had an important influence on the Israeli and Palestinian literatures that criticize the Zionist state'. Atef Botros al-Attar, who researches the Arab reception of Kafka, complicates the picture by pointing to 'eight decades of Arab preoccupation' with Kafka, which 'swings between fascination, iconization, and holiness on the one hand and accusation, skepticism and denunciation on the other', and quotes a line from Mahmoud Darwish, often regarded as Palestine's national poet, written after the Israeli siege of Beirut: 'I found Kafka sleeping just beneath my skin.' Jens Hanssen, a historian of the Middle East, argues that 'the stakes of reading Kafka in the contemporary Arab world' are even higher than Botros suggests: 'Kafka's work is part of the Arab political lexicon precisely because many Arabs feel they have experienced his fiction as reality.'

One of Hanssen's examples is Nayrouz Malek, a Syrian novelist who prominently featured Kafka in a 'daring work of regime criticism' from 2000, the year of the Damascus Spring. In a moment of personal and political crisis, Malek's protagonist immerses himself in Kafka's writing, to the point that, by the end of the story, he lives in a mental asylum under the name 'Kafka'. Before taking that step, he begins conversing with a statue of Kafka – in Arabic, which, the statue explains, it has decided to learn 'because, in their feverish fight against Zionism, some Arab critics accused me of being a Zionist and a writer who serves Zionist ideology', and it wanted to 'tell them that my position is the opposite of what they think'. This anti-Zionist Kafka is an anachronistic invention – and not even because of his actual views on Zionism, which were ambiguous, but because the type of Zionism he had views on, as he got to know it in the 1910s and 1920s in Prague, Vienna and Berlin, was a different movement from Zionism in the late twentieth and early twenty-first centuries. We simply cannot know what Kafka would have made of Zionist politics today.

And yet the desire to know – the desire to engage Kafka as an ally, or as an opponent, in relation to one's political agenda – is strong. To these readers, it clearly matters deeply what Kafka thought – and even more what he would have thought, had he lived longer. This is ultimately the gene-alogy of both Bruce's alternative history in which Kafka becomes the first Israeli Nobel Prize winner with a troubled relationship to the Arab–Israeli conflict, and Malek's resur-rected anti-Zionist statue, perhaps merely imagined by the troubled Syrian protagonist. More broadly, there is a clear tendency among Kafka's readers to adopt and deploy him in the conflicts of their own age, as we have already seen in Brexit-torn Britain, Communist Czechoslovakia and other contexts.

There are many factors at play here. The fact of Kafka's early death, combined with the unfinished state of most of his manuscripts, and the frequent ambiguity and play with paradoxes at the heart of his texts, invites rewritings and afterlives. His iconic status on the world literary scene prom-ises to bestow legitimacy on his self-appointed disciples; the reflected light of his celebrity might illuminate those who remain in the shadows. As we will see in Chapter Five, the 'Kafkaesque' has become a literary brand that can help sell and promote books, often in translation. But at the root of all these secondary reasons for Kafka's fame lies the rich tapestry of Kafka's mental and creative life, whose many threads sometimes seem to pull in different directions, though this complexity only adds to its appeal. We have already seen this in his relationship to the German language and culture, and his Czech environment. We will now see it in Kafka's attitude towards his Jewishness too.

Kafka's Jewishness

It has often been remarked that the word 'Jewish' does not appear anywhere in Kafka's literature – but it crops up again and again in his other writings, including his letters, where he often discusses his own identity, as well as various social issues facing Jewish people. These reflections are often ambiguous or contradictory, and change over time. They should not be reduced to a snippet from Kafka's diary from 1914, unconnected to the preceding and following notes in any obvious way, but often quoted on account of its tantalising brevity and decisiveness: 'What do I have in common with Jews? I have scarcely anything in common with myself and should stand completely silent in a corner, content that I can breathe.' The German word used here to express commonality – 'gemeinsam' – shares its root with the word 'Gemeinschaft', the 'community' that Kafka had so desperately longed for, according to Brod. As so often with Kafka, his comment comes across as both deeply serious, a record of discomfort, even pain – and quietly humorous: the dramatic exasperation of the opening rhetorical question; the tragicomedy of a man who has 'scarcely anything' in common with himself; the hyperbolic image of this anxious man standing in the corner like a naughty child.

Kafka's comment hides yet another duality. It posits the existence of a stable and uniform Jewish community of which Kafka is not a part – whereas, as he knew very well himself, in reality many different Jewish communities coexisted in his time, and the differences between them fascinated Kafka no end. In the next section, we will meet Puah Ben-Tovim, one of Kafka's Hebrew teachers, born and raised in Palestine, a representative of the first generation of native speakers of modern Hebrew. But we will start with people who were much closer to home, geographically speaking, and yet perceived as just as, if not even more, removed from the way of life of Kafka and his friends from Prague, Vienna and Berlin: the so-called 'Ostjuden', or Eastern European Jews.

The term 'Ostjuden' was used by German-speaking Jews to refer to Yiddish-speaking Jews living in various Eastern European countries, above all in Poland, where some 3 million Jewish people lived in the 1910s and 1920s. The linguistic difference was seen as crucial in this differentiation – all the more so given that the ancestors of most German-speaking Jews in Western Europe – including Kafka's family – used to speak Yiddish too, and the change to German was key to their social assimilation. To Kafka, the multilingual wordsmith that he was, the Yiddish language seemed fascinating.

When Kafka writes about Yiddish, he calls it 'Jargon'. This term initially struck me as surprising, since it sounds pejorative, but what Kafka has to say about it he clearly frames as positive – at least in comparison to the unabashed negativity espoused by other speakers of German. The language whose name only relatively recently, in the late nineteenth and early twentieth centuries, became standardised as 'yidish' – which also means 'Jewish' – was initially conceptualised by German speakers as a degraded form of German, often referred to as 'Judeo-German'. Some German-speaking Jews took up this negative rhetoric too. As Jeffrey Shandler explains in his book *Yiddish: Biography of a Language*, 'zhargon' was one of the most enduring terms for the language, even though it originated as a descriptor with decidedly negative connotations, 'either the inscrutable language of a closed group or a debased, uncivilized form of speech – in either case, something less than a full, proper language'. But the use of the term evolved over the years and in Kafka's time it was often used as a neutral descriptor. As Shandler shows, around the turn of the twentieth century it even appeared in the titles of several Yiddish-language textbooks. And yet even once it was to some extent reclaimed, the term 'Jargon' continued to encode centuries of oppression and discrimination faced by its speakers, especially at the hands of those who spoke the more prestigious neighbouring German.

Yiddish-speaking Jews were also often subject to hostile treatment in my own country, Poland, where they had lived since the Middle Ages and accounted for about 10 per cent of the population before the Second World War – the highest percentage in all of Europe. Ninety per cent of Polish Jews were murdered during the Holocaust, and very few survivors remained in Poland after the war. Growing up, I did not learn enough about this history. It was only after I moved to Britain and experienced life in a multicultural community here, with its tensions but above all its day-to-day richness, that I was able to better understand the extent to which the Holocaust, a total tragedy for its predominantly Jewish victims, was also a profound loss for Poland, which changed forever without its Jewish population. This sense of loss was expressed shortly before I emigrated in a project initiated by the activist and performer Rafał Betlejewski, who painted the phrase 'tęsknię za tobą, Żydzie' – 'I miss you, Jew' – in prominent public spaces around Poland.

Searching for Kafka's afterlives in Poland, I discovered that he has been co-opted for this nostalgic project of Poland's Jewish revival too. Remigiusz Grzela's *Franz K.'s Luggage:*

The Journey That Never Was (2004) recounts the stories of Polish Jews whom Kafka met and developed close relationships with – among them his last love Dora Diamant, actor Jizchak Löwy and other members of Löwy's Yiddish theatre troupe. Grzela's book was subsequently adapted as *Circus Kafka* at the Jewish Theatre in Warsaw, featuring 'the star of a Jewish-Czech-German-Polish variety show: Franz Kafka', who meets Dora Diamant and decides to move to Warsaw with her. But the play presents this 'Warszawa' ('Warsaw') as 'Niewarszawa' ('Notwarsaw'), marking the loss of Jewish lives, and Jewish cultural life, that all but disappeared from the Polish capital after the Second World War – and also imagines a 'Kafkopolis', where all the characters could live. Here we yet again encounter a fantasy of resurrection, but unlike in the texts by Bruce and Malek, Kafka is engaged not to think through Zionist politics in the Middle East in the decades after his death, but the politics of Poland's Jewish past.

From Yiddish to Hebrew

Kafka met Löwy in 1911, when Löwy's troupe toured in Prague. Many commentators disparaged their performances, which were done on the cheap, relied on rowdy humour and did not aspire to the prestige and self-importance of institutionalised repertory theatres. But Kafka was enthralled: in the autumn of 1911 and winter of 1912, detailed descriptions of the Yiddish shows he saw and the actors he met take up a large proportion of his notebooks. The most famous document from this time is a short speech Kafka gave before one of the troupe's performances in Prague. It is directed at the German-speaking spectators: or rather, listeners – for Kafka focuses on the experience of hearing the Yiddish language as a Jewish speaker of German.

'Before we come to the first poems by our Eastern Jewish poets, I should like, ladies and gentlemen, just to say something about how much more Jargon you understand than you think', Kafka begins. But this understanding is currently blocked by such a 'fear' of 'Jargon' that 'one can almost see it in your faces' – a fear 'mingled with a certain fundamental distaste'. What is the source of these ugly emotions? Kafka explicitly contrasts the 'order' of Jewish life in Western Europe with the 'confusion' of 'Jargon' – which, Kafka says, lacks sophisticated expressions and does not have a proper grammar, all on account of being the youngest European language. It consists exclusively of loan words from other languages, and the only 'language' that in turn borrows from it is thieves' argot; and in fact 'Jargon as a whole consists only of dialect'. 'Kafka's remarks on the nature of Yiddish', Shandler writes, 'are so laden with errors that they appear coyly deliberate.' I am not entirely persuaded by this charitable interpretation of Kafka's speech.

But first it is helpful, as Shandler does, to link Kafka's 'playfully contradictory' take on Yiddish to Freud's evocation of the language in his study *Jokes and Their Relation to the Unconscious* (1905), where it is associated with a repressed, 'true' Jewish self, whereas German represents the assimilated super-ego. Indeed, the core of Kafka's speech revolves around the fraught relationship between the two languages, which oscillates between familiarity and unfamiliarity, perhaps best captured by another of Freud's famous terms – the uncanny. Kafka says:

The links between Jargon and German are too deli-
cate and significant not to be torn to shreds the instant
Jargon is transformed back into German, that is to
say, it is no longer Jargon that is transformed, but
something that has utterly lost its essential character.
If it is translated into French, for instance, Jargon can
be conveyed to the French, but if it is translated into
German it is destroyed. 'Toit', for instance, is not the
same thing as 'tot' [dead], and 'blüt' is far from being
'blut' [blood].

The task that Kafka sets his listeners, then, is to try to
'understand Jargon intuitively'; 'if you stay still, you suddenly find yourselves in the midst of Jargon', he advises the
audience – 'and Jargon is everything, the words, the Chasidic
melody, and the essential character of this East European
Jewish actor himself', he explains. It will then become possible for a crucial shift to occur – 'it will frighten you, yet
it will no longer be fear of Jargon but of yourselves' – and
yet this experience of dwelling in 'Jargon' might inspire a
sense of 'self-confidence' that will allow the listeners to
overcome this fear. Kafka is engaging his audience's internalised anti-Semitic prejudice aimed specifically at speakers
of Yiddish to show them two things: first, that their fluency
in German does not ultimately insulate them from such
prejudice; and, second, that in attempting to insulate themselves from it, German-speaking, Westernised, assimilated
Jews lose something important – a connection to the rough-
hewn yet life-sustaining force of Yiddish, and with it Eastern
European Jewish life.

On one level, Kafka's speech is a circuitous attempt to

think his way out of internalised anti-Semitism. But on another level, I would suggest a different interpretation. In the 1990s, Serbian scholar Milica Bakić-Hayden coined the term 'nesting Orientalisms' to complicate Edward Said's famous theory of Orientalism by pointing out that even communities that are themselves subject to orientalisation by others can in turn orientalise another group. In Chapter Two, we saw how Kafka was orientalised by some German readers more securely ensconced in Western Europe on account of his proximity to the 'spiritual' and 'wild' East of Europe; now we see how Kafka himself speaks of Eastern European Jews in similar terms, fetishising the supposed 'simplicity' and 'authenticity' of their culture and way of life. Kafka claims to speak of it in admiration – but it is still a form of othering.

It was not just Yiddish that fascinated Kafka with its tantalising promise of access to a different realm of Jewish experience: he went on to develop an interest in Hebrew too. One winter day, I arrange to meet in the Bodleian Library with a colleague who researches modern Hebrew literature. We are here to look at Kafka's Hebrew notebooks. Except that we are not allowed to look at the actual notebooks – they are far too fragile – and instead are headed to a designated computer in the corner of the reading room. You need a special password; we have the special password. There is only one folder on the desktop. It contains high-resolution photographs of the individual pages of all of Kafka's notebooks kept in Oxford, including all the blank pages too, as well as a number of loose sheets and even mere scraps of paper.

Hunched over the screen, we begin by pulling up MS. Kafka 33, a notebook that has never before been published or even transcribed, except, perhaps, for private use by scholars who have visited the library over the years. All we know is that there is some writing in Hebrew in there, and a little drawing on the inside cover: an upside-down, amorphous, squiggly shape, with a bald, oval head and slits for eyes and nose. A 'ghostlike figure', according to Andreas Kilcher, who has recently meticulously collated all known drawings by Kafka in a lavish coffee-table edition – some impressive sketches, but mostly doodles, squiggles and scribbles. Since Kafka noted the Hebrew term 'guardian of the threshold' or 'doorkeeper' on the first page of the notebook, Kilcher conjectures that the drawing illustrates this resonant and yet ultimately elusive concept, often evoking suspension between life and death. He dates the notebook to 1923, when Kafka's health was deteriorating so fast that he knew he was approaching this particular threshold. But his ghostly doorkeeper also guards the gateway that leads from German to Hebrew. After one final look at this strange creature, we dive into the world of Kafka's Hebrew notebooks.

Hebrew Notebooks

As a life-long language learner, I am strangely moved because what I see is so familiar. Most pages are filled with vocab lists: two columns per page, with Hebrew words on the right and German words on the left. From time to time, there are longer phrases, sometimes a sentence or two, or a verb with its attendant conjugations. The German is relatively easy to read, but we struggle with the Hebrew: the writing is uncertain, idiosyncratic – except for a few pages of homework, where Kafka clearly tried hard to produce his best Hebrew penmanship.

The vocabulary is advanced, my colleague points out. From time to time we do come across quite elementary words, but of course every language learner knows the frustration of forgetting the most basic expressions as you are already working hard to master difficult grammar, or – even worse – realising that you had not known that simple phrase in the first place. Language learning keeps you in check: you never sound as smart, articulate and knowledge-able as you would like to, or think you should. But that does not stop you from trying – and Kafka relished every opportunity to practise his Hebrew. In the spring of 1920, for example, just a few days after his arrival to take a cure in the South Tyrolean resort of Meran, Kafka jumps at the chance to 'exchange my scanty words of Hebrew' with a 'Turkish-Jewish rug dealer', 'an intimate friend of the chief rabbi of Constantinople'.

I take a moment to imagine what sort of conversation with this rug dealer, or one of his teachers, Kafka might have tried to build around the words he scribbled in the note-books now kept in the Bodleian. My favourite example is the page where, one after another, we find the following words: 'canary bird', 'because of', 'to sleep badly'. You can just imagine Kafka attempting to complain in Hebrew about his disrupted night and difficult morning, as he often does in German in his diaries and letters. Or perhaps he is trying to explain his daily routine – an exercise familiar to any language learner. He notes down words for 'washba-sin', 'earlier', 'usual', 'exception'. With your language skills stripped down to an intermediate level, which is where Kafka's Hebrew will have been at, you stick to the hard facts. I usually sleep badly. I wake up late and wash my face in a washbasin before going to work. And there is Gregor Samsa of course, with his 'unsettled dreams': with the vocabulary on this two-page spread, Kafka could have just about had a stab at summarising the opening sentences of *The Metamorphosis* in Hebrew.

Skipping between the pages, we discover lots of lovely little details. There are snippets of Czech, French and Italian: a reminder of Kafka's multilingualism beyond German and Hebrew. Other pages turn out to be unexpectedly poignant. At one point, Kafka writes down the words for 'thermometer', 'degrees (of fever)' and a skeleton of a longer sentence: 'I am too tired to'. His illness was progressing fast.

Then there is a loose leaf on which Kafka wrote a letter to one of his teachers, Puah Ben-Tovim, in 1923. My colleague lingers over it; it is her favourite bit of Hebrew in the whole collection. Ben-Tovim is one of the most intriguing figures in Kafka's life. She was born in Jerusalem in a Hebrew-speaking family in 1903, which made her one of the earliest native speakers of modern Hebrew. In the late nineteenth and early twentieth centuries, the sacred language of the Bible was being adapted for daily use in Palestine; from the 1880s, some Jewish parents who grew up speaking other languages themselves began to raise their children using this vernacular form of Hebrew instead.

Ben-Tovim came to Prague in 1921, upon finishing at a German-language school in Jerusalem, to take up university studies in mathematics; she would go on to become a teacher in Israel. She was eighteen when she arrived in Prague, where a local rabbi suggested she volunteer as a teacher of modern Hebrew. Among her students: one Franz Kafka. 'At the time that name meant nothing to me', Ben-Tovim reminisced decades later. She was surprised to discover that Kafka had already been learning Hebrew since 1917.

'Kafka looked weak, so weak.' Of course he did: by the time Ben-Tovim met him in 1922, his tuberculosis was already very advanced. But that was not all. She continues seamlessly: 'The effects of his illness were additionally compounded by his difficulties with women. I gradually learned some details about these.' Might this explain how the words for 'fiancée', 'betrothal' and 'four times' made it on to a page of a notebook from 1923, even though we only know of Kafka's three engagements? In any case, this was a somewhat alarming setup: Kafka was twice Ben-Tovim's age, and she complained about her older male pupils accosting her. But she does not seem to have counted Kafka among the men who made her uncomfortable. He was reserved and very polite, she says: often complimented her on her appearance, once declared that her confidence appealed to him, but she 'did not detect any erotic tension' between the two of them. Then again: 'He was undeniably attracted to me, but more to an ideal than the real girl I was: to the image of the faraway Jerusalem, about which he kept asking me, and where he wanted to accompany me on my return.'

In the short letter we are looking at in the Bodleian, Kafka attempts to comfort Ben-Tovim, who is anxiously awaiting a letter from Jerusalem, from her parents, who disapprove of her plan to continue her studies in Berlin. So much of this must have resonated with Kafka: disapproving parents? Desire to move to Berlin? Anxiety about a pending letter? That was the very stuff of the man's life! No wonder that the situation motivated him to carefully write out his Hebrew letters much more neatly than in his usual notes. Despite some shaky grammar and an occasional awkward vocabulary choice, the letter is both funny and moving. Kafka starts by recounting the facts of the situation, and then warms up to his subject:

> I well understand the chaos one often feels when waiting for a decisive letter that is lost somewhere. I have felt the same anxiety many times in my life. It's a wonder that nobody turns to ash earlier than they actually do. I'm sorry that you are suffering so much, poor, dear Puah, meanwhile the letter has come and everything is all right now.

Few readers of Kafka will be familiar with this charming Hebrew letter, though: Kafka's Hebrew writings are the only manuscripts of his that have not been published yet, except for a few scattered excerpts. They are set to appear as the last volume of the critical edition of Kafka's work published by S. Fischer Verlag in Germany, which has been listed as forthcoming for several decades now. That is why the thrill of seeing Kafka's Hebrew notebooks in the Bodleian, even on a computer screen, is so palpable – both for me, a scholar of Kafka who does not know Hebrew, and my colleague, who does not work on Kafka but has dedicated her life to the study of Hebrew.

The Hebrew Notebook

As excited as both of us are to be reading these notebooks, we are still quite a far way off from the most striking account of encountering Kafka's Hebrew that I have come across.

This distinction belongs to Ruth Kanner, professor of theatre arts at Tel Aviv University and director of an experimental theatre group. In 2013 – during the ongoing trial over the ownership of Kafka's manuscripts – Kanner was invited by the director of the National Library of Israel to produce an artistic response to a chosen book from its collections to celebrate the 120th anniversary of the institution. Here is Freddie Rokem's English translation of the Hebrew monologue performed by an actress playing Kanner at the beginning of the play that Kanner created in response to that call:

> I went to the library. I was looking for something that would be of interest to me, but didn't find anything. I was on the verge of giving up . . . and then – just like that – without any real expectations I asked the archivist – perhaps, by any chance – you do have there something hidden on . . . of . . . probably not . . . 'cause everything has been published and said but . . . perhaps . . . yet . . . you have by any chance something in the archives of . . . Franz Kafka??? And he said: yes . . . and went underground – that is where they hide all of their special treasures in safes – and came back with a thin, blue notebook and put it in my hands!!! I am holding in my hands a notebook that Franz Kafka himself wrote! His own handwriting! I didn't know what to do with it – I smelled it! I wanted to eat it!!!

As soon as I come across a description of this play, titled *The Hebrew Notebook*, and its opening monologue bursting with frenzied energy, I am determined to find a way to watch it: here I will have a unique chance to experience an intense, emotional encounter with one of Kafka's Hebrew notebooks, very similar to those I saw in the Bodleian, from the perspective of an Israeli speaker of Hebrew.

Much to my delight, a helpful member of Kanner's theatre company arranges for me to watch a recording of the play on Zoom. One winter morning I sit down at the dining room table and open up my laptop. It is a very strange experience: separated from the play by a language barrier, two computer screens, the lens of the camera, several years and many miles, I nevertheless find it captivating. The visceral fascination with one of Kafka's small blue notebooks communicates itself clearly even through all those layers of distance: I feel like I am sniffing it myself, and want to chew on it too! The play encourages such appetite for individual words: as audience members pass from the foyer, where the opening monologue was held, to the main theatre hall, everyone is handed their own little flashcard with one of Kafka's German–Hebrew vocabulary pairs.

Kafka had often been subjected to a similar treatment by scholars: not just close reading, but painstaking word-by-word analysis. In his biography of Kafka, Brod went as far as to proclaim that his friend never wrote a 'single word' that was not 'infused with a special magic charm'. The Hebrew notebooks lend themselves to such an approach both less – and more. Less because they are not literary texts; more because these are actual word lists, and the words listed here are arguably central to Kafka's life and work. This, at least, is the argument implicitly made in Ruth Kanner's play. One word the actors conjugate on stage, for example, is the Hebrew verb 'radaf' – to 'chase' or 'pursue'. This recitation is followed by a simple staging of two short texts by Kafka, 'An Old Manuscript' and 'Jackals and Arabs', both of which describe territorial conflicts between two different communities. As Freddie Rokem, professor in the department of theatre studies at Tel Aviv University, explains, by the end of the play 'the audience is transported from the world of individual words and their associative potentials to the disturbing narratives of conflict where the words now serve the development of the story'.

By linking Kafka's acquisition of individual words in a new language with his German storytelling, *The Hebrew Notebook* focuses our attention on the process by which Kafka's German-language writing would develop out of scattered notes. Not unlike his Hebrew notebooks, Kafka's diaries also often feature short phrases, even individual, disjointed words: snippets of thought, or expressions he heard or read somewhere; half-finished sentences, often deliciously suggestive of a story that could emerge out of them.

But unlike many of my colleagues and other readers, I have to confess that I do not particularly enjoy reading Kafka's diaries. A lot of what is in them is extremely mundane – unadorned records of who Kafka saw and where they went, what the people he saw looked like, how much (or – more often – little) he slept – or plainly off-putting: much self-pity about what sound like quite petty incidents, extremely banal sexism in descriptions of women, unkind remarks about this or that friend or family member, detailed descriptions of dreams which, just like – let us be frank – most dreams, lose quite a bit of their suggestive power in the retelling. The diaries do yield much interesting factual information about his life, but the efforts at reconstructing Kafka's psychology and character based on them often seem to fall flat. Isolated remarks, contradicted at other places, are inflated to grotesque proportions; a lot is made of what were plainly throwaway comments. Kafka would be truly mortified at the thought of strangers reading and analysing his diaries in this way, and I feel like a voyeur each time I pick up a volume.

Writing the Body

But there are a few good bits in the diaries, of course, and almost always the reason I enjoy them is that Kafka manages to gradually transform what starts as another display of obsessive self-pity into gentle comedy. Take this passage, from November 1911, several years before any externally observable decline in his health. But Kafka strikes an earnest, despairing tone and, in hindsight, knowing what awaits him – he will eventually cough up blood, dramatically lose weight, die tragically young – it is hard not to take his complaints seriously:

> There's no doubt that a main obstacle to my progress is my physical condition. With such a body nothing can be achieved. I will have to get used to its perpetual failure. From the last few wildly dreamed-through but barely even snatchily slept-through nights I was so incoherent this morning, felt nothing but my forehead, saw a halfway bearable condition only far beyond the present one . . .

But then, without warning, something shifts and, seemingly in the little space between one clause and another,

Kafka stops taking himself so seriously: 'and in sheer read-
iness for death at one point [I] would have liked to curl up
with the documents in my hand on the cement tiles of the
corridor.' This is such a comically pathetic image – the office
papers in his hand! the exact description of the office floor!
– that the first time I read it I just burst out with uncontrollable laughter. Which, by the by, is what often happened
when Kafka read out from his writing to his friends. Yes,
even the supposedly chillingly dystopian *Trial*. Many
readers over the decades have cast Kafka as a prophet of
twentieth-century totalitarianisms: his works seemed to
powerfully resonate with the violent and oppressive aber-
rations of bureaucratic systems employed to persecute and
destroy whole populations, including Kafka's own Jewish
relatives. But Kafka himself died in 1924, while Hitler was
still in prison and the Nazi Party had not yet started its elec-
toral ascent, and Stalin had only just assumed power in the
Soviet Union after Lenin's death. Despite all the tensions
mounting in Europe in the early twentieth century, Kafka
did not live in a dystopian nightmare. And despite his poor
health and dissatisfaction with his day job, by all accounts
he was a pleasant, funny man.

In the November 1911 passage from the diary, Kafka is
leaning into his comedic lamentation. 'My body is too long
for its weakness', he observes, and he means *literally* too
long – a smidge under six feet, so markedly tall for the age:

How is the weak heart, which recently has often stabbed
me, supposed to push the blood down the whole length
of these legs. To the knee would be enough work, but
then it is washed with only decrepit strength into the

cold lower legs. But now it is already needed again up above, one waits for it while it dissipates down below.

Kafka writes the body so well: with so much keenly observed detail, so much unexpected comedy, such a verve, a sense of vitality hilariously antithetical to the feebleness he describes. In November 1911, Kafka is in thrall of the Yiddish troupe touring in Prague; he jots down copious notes about the expressive acting style of its actors, in which he sees a joyous vigour, a zest for life. In his diary, Kafka translates what he sees on the stage into a tragicomedy of his own body. In the title of his influential interpretation of Kafka's oeuvre from 1995, Sander Gilman – a prominent scholar of German literature, psychoanalysis and history of medicine – dubbed Kafka 'the Jewish patient': Kafka's relationship with his own body, expressed in his body of writing, the argument goes, needs to be understood in the context of the contemporary anti-Semitic discourse about the male Jewish body as ethnically distinctive, effeminate and prone to disease.

But it would be reductive to equate Kafka's literary engagement with the body with his Jewishness. Here it is instructive to take a look at one of the few free-standing pieces which Kafka published in newspapers and magazines during his life, having first drafted them in his diary, where notes about everyday events, encounters and reflections are interspersed with literary drafts. In this case, we get a paragraph that seems to belong in both categories simultaneously, or provide as perfect a bridge between the two as anywhere in Kafka's work. He composed 'Great Noise', the little text I have in mind, just a couple of weeks before the passage cited above. It is clearly autobiographical – Valli, mentioned halfway through, was the name used in the family for one of Kafka's sisters, Valerie – and we know from many other passages in the diaries how sensitive Kafka was to noise, including the singing of the family's canary birds, so bothersome that they made it on to his Hebrew vocabulary list years later. But, as so often with him, an everyday situation is gradually, almost stealthily, transformed into a striking image decidedly literary in character, with an uncanny bodily transformation at its centre:

> I'm sitting in my room in the headquarters of the noise of the whole apartment. I hear all the doors banging, their noise spares me only the footsteps of those running between them, I hear even the slam of the oven door in the kitchen. My father bursts through the doors of my room and passes through in his dragging dressing gown, the ashes are being scraped out of the stove in the next room, Valli asks shouting into the indefinite through the hall whether Father's hat has been cleaned yet, a hiss that wants to be my friend raises the cry of an answering voice. The apartment door is unlatched and makes a noise as if from a catarrhal throat, then continues to open with the brief singing of a woman's voice and closes with a dull manly jerk that sounds the most inconsiderate of all. My father is gone, now begins the gentler more scattered more hopeless noise, led by the voices of the two canaries. I thought of it before, but with the canaries it occurs to me anew, whether I shouldn't open the door a little crack, crawl like a snake into the next room and thus on the floor ask my sisters and their governess for quiet.

Kafka wrote this piece in the apartment that became the model for the Samsa family's apartment in *The Metamorphosis*. His room was located in between his sisters' room and his parents' bedroom, which meant that they had to walk through his room to get to theirs. Three doors in total led to his room: he truly did occupy 'the headquarters of the noise of the whole apartment'. But it is as though the noise coming from all these places, which would normally disturb Kafka's writing, in this case dramatically tips over and opens up a fount of creativity, which allows Kafka to spit out this evocative vignette, which will resonate with every writer, or anybody who works at a desk and is often disturbed by the banging of doors, endless chatter of others, sounds from kitchens, endless boiling of water for tea, endless clattering of cups.

As befits the description of a space that would ultimately inspire Kafka's greatest story of human-to-animal transformation, a central element of 'Great Noise' is the image hinted at in its last sentence. The narrator imagines – not for the first time – sneaking out through a crack in the door 'like a snake' – in German it is just one word, 'schlangengleich' – and pleading his sisters to stay quiet. This is a striking image with connotations that seem to pull in different directions. On the one hand, a snake is the embodiment of silence: it can only hiss, never speak, and its movement is soundless. On the other hand, a snake is a dangerous threat: it can bite or suffocate you. The narrator's fantasy of a self-effacing plea for silence, then, contains a seed of a silent threat.

Reading Trials

Kafka's three novels also emerge out of fragmentary drafts scattered across his notebooks. I have already looked at *The Trial* in Chapter One to understand the role that the Oxford scholar Malcolm Pasley played in editing this novel for the German critical edition of Kafka's works. But it is also worth examining the novel from another perspective, taking as the starting point the almost obligatory comparisons made between *The Trial* and the 'Kafkaesque' trial over Kafka's manuscripts in Jerusalem, and reflecting more broadly on how the use of the term 'Kafkaesque' to describe convoluted, anxiety-inducing bureaucratic processes relates to the actual content of *The Trial*.

I first read the novel in the summer after my first year of university. Reading in German was a skill I was still practising, and Kafka is often recommended as a good entry point, on account of his limpid syntax and largely everyday vocabulary. This is a world of doors, windows, staircases, coats, shirts, horse riding, dogs, maids, villagers and judges, rather than sculpted façades, stained glass, foyers, silk-lined surtouts, starched shirtfronts, equestrian sports, poodles, governesses, town councillors and grain merchants – the type of precise, refined vocabulary that one might encounter in, say, Thomas Mann. Here the seeds of the first reason for the associative power of the term 'Kafkaesque' are to be found: the contrast between the lucidity of Kafka's language and the murkiness of his plots.

Even so, there were still plenty of new words to learn from *The Trial*. I devised a special system to assimilate them: I would listen to a German audiobook of the novel and follow along in a physical book containing the Polish translation. I soon discovered that this was not a fool-proof plan, as the two versions did not really match up. It seemed that some episodes were told in a different order, or entirely missing from one version but present in the other. Was this a problem with my Polish translation? Was my German not good enough to follow? Or was I having some sort of, dare I say, Kafkaesque experience with the novel? No: I was merely discovering a key fact about much of Kafka's writing. There is no one definitive version of it.

Kafka drafted *The Trial* in 1914 and 1915, but never published it – although a short excerpt, which we encountered in Chapter Three, was published under the title 'Before the Law'. But Brod thought that this unfinished novel was a masterpiece that would posthumously put Kafka on the map, and so he edited it for publication in 1925, a year after Kafka's death. This involved standardising Kafka's spelling and punctuation, arranging chapters and fragments scattered across various notebooks into a coherent sequence, excising a number of unfinished sections, and framing Kafka's writings as deeply religious, fundamentally Jewish texts: as we have seen in Chapter Three, during his friend's lifetime he already described them as 'the most Jewish documents of our time'. Brod has been much criticised over the years for his editorial interventions, especially once Germanists got their hands on the manuscript decades later and new critical editions were produced – a process in which Oxford's Malcolm Pasley played a leading role. But the assessment of Brod's editorial role needs more nuance. Kafka himself adjusted his spelling and punctuation when publishing other texts during his lifetime, and would have been horrified at the thought of seeing unfinished sentences and broken-off chapters in print.

Today, after a century of dramatic developments in aesthetic norms and tastes, fuelled not in the least by the growing appreciation of tortured modernists like Kafka, many readers might be much more comfortable with such writing, praising it as pushing the boundaries of literary convention – much more comfortable than Kafka *himself*, who despaired at his inability to neatly wrap up his plots. Things were different in 1925. In order for Kafka, a writer of some acclaim but uncertain status mere months after his early death, to become Kafka, the global icon of literary modernity, Brod needed people to *read* him, and for that he needed a *readable novel*: a longer book, not just a short story or a collection of short pieces; one with a clear beginning and end and an intelligible middle, and a compelling, substantial interpretation that would put the visionary character of Kafka's writing beyond any doubt. And that is what Brod achieved at the time.

The Trial begins with another of Kafka's famous opening sentences, rivalled only by *The Metamorphosis*. 'Someone must have been telling tales about Josef K., for one morning, without having done anything wrong, he was arrested.' Part of what is so striking about this sentence – aside from the strong emotional reaction it is likely to elicit in any reader who has ever felt unjustly accused, or extremely defensive about their behaviour – is its strange perspectival mismatch. There is a strong sense that what we have verbalised here is the protagonist's own train of thought – well, I've done nothing wrong, but I was just arrested, so somebody must have said something untrue about me! At the same time, having him identified as 'Josef K.' gives the sentence the ominous ring of a newspaper report on a high-profile arrest.

The issue of Josef K.'s guilt is never resolved in the novel one way or another – we never really get a satisfactory answer as to what Josef K. might have done, or how he had come to the attention of the authorities – and this has, understandably, frustrated some readers and pushed others to propose a whole host of interpretations. Some have seen the novel as a giant, sprawling metaphor for the metaphysical guilt we all carry, in the Christian – but not Jewish – tradition associated with the original sin. Others have suggested that Josef K. had not done anything wrong, but merely manoeuvred himself into the whole mess to fulfil some sort of dark, unconscious psychological need to be judged, and punished. The seeds of both these interpretations are already there in the first sentence. But I am particularly partial to another sentence on the first page of the novel, a little further down, and much easier to overlook – and yet one that offers an opportunity to arrive at an alternative definition of the 'Kafkaesque', one which I find more helpful and more precise at capturing the textual mechanics of Kafka's literary world.

It is the description of the clothes worn by one of the unknown men who come to arrest Josef K. that fateful morning: 'a close-fitting black suit which, like an outfit for travelling, was equipped with a variety of pleats, pockets, buckles, buttons, and a belt that made it appear especially practical, without its precise purpose being clear.' This, really, is Kafka 101: a prominently placed, painstakingly detailed description of an object whose significance is not immediately obvious – as explicitly stated in a series of strategically placed subclauses. A grammatical indication of logical causation: check (the German sentence includes a clever little word 'infolgedessen', which translates as 'as a result of this'). A confident assertion of meaning: check ('especially practical'). A subtle undermining of that very assertion, and the logical causation, in more than one way: check, check ('made it appear' rather than simply 'made it'; 'without its precise purpose being clear').

Kafka's world is full of such objects that appear exceedingly practical, as though some competent person were about to step in and calmly operate them in a way that would make their deeper purpose – and not just the superficial mechanism – super obvious. But in Kafka's world, such persons never materialise. And that is what 'Kafkaesque' really means to me.

Travelling On

I began this book in Oxford, right where most of Kafka's surviving manuscripts are kept, the place from which – both literally and metaphorically – I read him. I then travelled all around Europe, to different places where Kafka lived or visited: Prague, Berlin, Vienna, Zurich and more. I spent time poring over Kafka's relationship to Judaism, Jewishness, Hebrew, Yiddish, Zionism – and Palestine, about which he fantasised much at various points in his life. Moving through all these places, whether physically or – like Kafka himself – in my imagination, I tried to disentangle various strands of Kafka's identity, life and writing, but ultimately wanted to show how and why we need to resist the urge to see these strands as separate, let alone mutually exclusive elements.

In the next chapter, we will move beyond places with a clear, tangible connection to Kafka, and venture further afield. Not only has Kafka become a global phenomenon, translated, published, read, adapted and discussed on every continent (perhaps except Antarctica, although if you are or know of a reader who has taken their copy of Kafka to the South Pole, do let me know!), but his own life and work need to be understood in a global context too. He had family, friends and work contacts in many different places around the world, and he wrote numerous texts and fragments set in foreign countries, often bearing real names but possessing imaginary characteristics.

I could have chosen to take you from Jerusalem back to Western Europe, especially France. Not only did Kafka himself travel to Paris, a well-thumbed copy of Gustave Flaubert's *Sentimental Education* (1869) – his favourite novel – in hand; here his works would also be read and interpreted in dramatically influential ways very early on, including by Jean-Paul Sartre and Albert Camus, who saw Kafka as a proto-existentialist. John T. Hamilton's ingeniously titled *France/Kafka: An Author in Theory* reveals that a whole host of other prominent thinkers in France was deeply affected by Kafka's writing too. Franz emerges as a foremost object of desire in France's passionate affair with philosophical discourse.

And what about Southern Europe – especially Italy? Kafka visited several picturesque destinations in the north of the country – at the time some of them were still in the Austro-Hungarian Empire – including Lake Garda, Milan and Venice. He returned to the region several times between 1909 and 1913, and again in 1920, first with Brod, later alone. In 1909, Kafka even published an entertaining newspaper report from an early air show he had seen in Italy, which featured Louis Blériot – who had just become the first aviator to fly over the English Channel – as well as, in the audience, the venerable Decadent Gabriele d'Annunzio. 'Il Profeta' still begrudged Kafka's irreverent description of him two decades later. By then, Kafka's works were already being translated and read in Italy. In fact, a recent book dubs a whole host of influential Italian writers of the twentieth century, from Italo Calvino to Elena Ferrante, 'Kafka's Italian Progeny'.

I could have also chosen to take you to North America – both Kafka's fantastical 'Amerika', the setting of *The Man who Disappeared*, and the real-life United States, where a German Jewish exile, Salman Schocken, published influential English editions of Kafka's works right after the Second World War. The English translations he used dated back to the 1930s, when Willa Muir, a Scottish writer, came across Kafka's work when travelling in Central Europe with her husband Edwin. But it was only when the Muirs' translations were republished in New York that they unleashed a wave of fascination with Kafka in the English-speaking world. Here they made it into the hands of the likes of Vladimir Nabokov, Orson Welles, Philip Roth and Woody Allen. Nabokov, the consummate entomologist, was much exercised by the question of what species Gregor Samsa transforms into, as we can tell from drawings he left in his copy. Welles might have shot his famous film adaptation of *The Trial* (1962) in Europe, but Anthony Perkins's Joseph K. is unmistakably American. In Roth's novels and Allen's films, motifs from Kafka abound, often as vehicles for their characters' sexual frustrations. In *The Breast* (1972), Roth has his male protagonist transform into a giant – you guessed it – breast.

From North America, we could have travelled south. Kafka fantasised about moving to South America at one point, but even if he never made it there himself, he ended up enthusiastically taken up by the magical realists of the so-called Latin American 'boom'. Jorge Luis Borges claimed to have read Kafka already in the 1910s, when he was learning German in Switzerland. The National Library of Argentina recently tracked down a copy of Borges's annotated copy of *The Man who Disappeared* from the 1930s. More figurative traces of his reading of Kafka can be found all over his fictional universe, not least in 'The Lottery in Babylon' (1941), a story of an indecipherable institution – or Company, with a capital 'C' – governing the lives of fictional Babylonians, who believe that one of the secret places where one can gain access to the Company is 'a sacred latrine called Qaphqa'.

The Stakes of Travel

In other places the experience of reading Kafka is much more fraught. In one of his stories, 'A Report to an Academy', an ape from the Gulf of Guinea gives a speech to a scientific society explaining how he learnt to imitate – literally 'ape' – his European captors to regain his freedom. Seloua Luste Boulbina, a philosopher and theorist of decolonisation, draws on this and other texts by Kafka in her book *Kafka's Monkey and Other Phantoms of Africa*, which – starting from its very title – draws attention to the fact that Kafka's writings do not ever offer access to Africa as such, but rather to European colonialist ideologies. She finds him a useful ally in untangling their workings.

Similarly, Mark Christian Thompson uncovers in Kafka a sustained reflection on Blackness – and points out how significant it is 'for an African-American scholar to intervene in Kafka studies': 'I am sometimes directly asked, Why do you do that? Wouldn't you prefer to stick with African-American authors? Always implied in this is *where you belong*.' For Thompson, reading Kafka is an opportunity to both think about race and resist racialised models of belonging. Other readers of colour have found different ways of intervening in Kafka's literary world. A. Igoni Barrett's *Blackass* (2015) features an epigraph from Kafka's *Metamorphosis* and opens with the Nigerian protagonist's discovery upon waking up one morning that he had turned white – except for one body part, irreverently indicated in the novel's title. Kafka's famous gambit is transformed here into a vehicle for exploring contemporary race relations. In Mohammed Said Hjiouij's *Kafka in Tangier* (2019), recently translated from Arabic into English, this very same gambit is unashamedly exploited as a ploy to catch readers' attention. The book begins thus:

He read Kafka's *Metamorphosis* before bed. When he woke up the next morning after a night of unsettling dreams, he found himself transformed in his bed into a monster. No, not a large insect like Gregor Samsa. More like a putrid and distorted version of himself. Nevertheless, he knew that his fate would be no different from that of young Samsa: he would die in three months, no more and no less, just before his twenty-seventh birthday.

Good. Now that I've caught your attention, let's go back to the beginning and proceed one step at a time.

With this opening, Hjiouij's narrator playfully capitalises on both the popularity and prestige associated with Kafka's work all around the world, using him as a device to secure the attention of the reader, which he might not otherwise be confident of.

Indeed, it may be more challenging to find places where Kafka did not experience a range of localised afterlives than those where he did. I recently came across *Mr K Released*, Matéi Visniec's 2010 novel which reflects on Romania's transition to democracy by using a figure borrowed from *The Trial*. The novel was brought out in English by a publishing house from India. There, Kafka has been translated into Hindi, Bengali, Tamil, Malayalam, Urdu and Gujarati, among other Indian languages, and 'is often interpreted with a local colour and adapted for current contexts' in India, explains Rosy Singh, a professor of German in New Delhi, where *The Trial* was recently adapted for the stage with Josef K. appearing as Kumar, a software engineer. Another play, this time in Pune in western India, put Kafka into conversation with Kabir Das, a fifteenth-century mystic poet. In Southeast Asia, Kafka is being read and transformed too – or 'unfolded', as in the title of the biennial Unfolding Kafka Festival, the first of which took place in Bangkok in 2015. It was initiated by Jitti Chompee, a dancer and choreographer. Its performances and installations explored the bending and doubling over of the human body as well as origami, the Japanese art of paper folding, to translate Kafka's texts into other media.

This ceaseless, stubborn shapeshifting holds the clues to the real value of Kafka's writing. He is the patron saint of creativity, of unobvious, unexpected connections, of fascination with complexity and paradoxes which cannot be ever fully explained or assimilated but can be unfolded and refolded in ever new combinations and constellations, both as a source of intellectual stimulation and of visceral pleasure. The unassuming man from Prague travels on. With the origami cicadas at the heart of 'The Silence of Insects', the interactive light installation staged at the Kafka festival in Bangkok by Yoko Seyama, a Japanese multimedia artist based in Berlin, we have extended the geography of Kafka's readership to East Asia. There are many avid readers of Kafka in the region today, not just in Japan, but also – as we are about to see – China and Korea.

5

Seoul

Asian Kafka

Kafka Arrives in East Asia

Haruki Murakami's bestselling Japanese novel *Kafka on the Shore* is now almost eclipsing the popularity of Kafka himself, not least in Google searches. While it might seem insignificant to mention a fact about a search engine, in this case technology allows us to track a shift in what readers associate with the brand Kafka today. Elif Batuman once advised readers of *Time* magazine in a 'What to Read This Summer' section: 'I was trying to read Kafka, but it turns out that Kafka is not great beach reading. Then the Kindle Web page had the brilliant idea that I should switch to Haruki Murakami's *Kafka on the Shore*. It was so right! The book isn't so much about Kafka, but it went perfectly with the shore.' But there is in fact much Kafka in Murakami's writing, and he is one of the winners of the international Franz Kafka Prize.

The protagonist of his 2013 short story 'Samsa in Love', for one, is an insect who wakes up and finds that it now inhabits the body of a man – and not just any man, but specifically one Gregor Samsa. This clumsy human, used to life as an insect, must teach himself to move and behave in new ways, and eventually falls in love – that most human emotional state. Not unlike Karl Brand, Kafka's tubercular contemporary from Prague who published a story about Gregor Samsa's 'retransformation', Murakami imagines an alternative, more hopeful ending for Kafka's tortured protagonist: a moment of connection in place of everlasting isolation. *Kafka on the Shore* signals its relationship with the famous predecessor and his literary brand too. The jackdaw stationery used by the Kafkas' fancy goods store in Prague reappears in spectral form on the cover and flyleaf of the first Japanese edition of the book: a faint, barely visible and yet unmistakeable and prominently placed reproduction of the characteristic design.

Kafka himself admired another set of Prague-meets-Tokyo designs when Emil Orlik, a visual artist from Prague who had just returned from a stay in Japan, exhibited his Japan-inspired prints and gave lectures on Japanese art in Prague in 1902. Ten years later, Orlik travelled to China; upon his return, he created lithograph illustrations for a collection of Chinese stories in a German translation. By then, Kafka had already started reading Chinese literature in German; one of his favourite books was Hans Heilmann's translation of a selection of Chinese poems spanning several centuries, published in 1905. The question of how to characterise and evaluate such mediated encounters with what at the time was commonly thought of in Europe as an undifferentiated, much mythologised but also disparaged 'Orient' – the name of a Prague cinema Kafka frequented – and in particular their impact on Kafka's literary imagination, has occupied many scholars over the years.

While Kafka was certainly not immune to Orientalist

stereotypes of his day, his engagement with Chinese culture also went beyond them. In 1912, for example, he quoted a poem from the Qing Dynasty he particularly liked, 'In the Dead of Night' by Yuan Mei, in a letter to Felice Bauer:

In the cold night, while poring over my book,
I forgot the hour of bedtime.
The scent of my gold-embroidered bedcover
Has already evaporated,
The fire in the hearth burns no more.
My beautiful mistress, who hitherto has controlled
Her wrath with difficulty, snatches away the lamp,
And asks: Do you know how late it is?

Kafka keeps coming back to this poem in several letters over the course of a few months. He appends Heilmann's commentary on the poem's author; contrasts it with other poems in the anthology; discusses the theme of a bookworm scholar; draws on both similarities and differences between the situation and figures in the poem and his own situation and relationship with Bauer. And yet in another message to her, sent while on an enjoyable holiday, Kafka includes a throwaway comment where China figures as little more than an unspecific faraway locale: 'I imagine if I were Chinese and were about to go home (indeed I am Chinese and I am going home), I would make sure of returning soon, and at any price.' As Rolf J. Goebel, the author of a seminal monograph on Kafka and China, points out, 'compared to his careful and detailed readings of Chinese poetry, Kafka's casual identification with an unspecified Chinese alter ego is strangely ambiguous, indeterminate, and non-committal'.

But even if Kafka's interest in Chinese culture had its limits, this does not appear to have limited his popularity in China. Yanbing Zeng, a scholar from the Renmin University of China, observes in his recent book that Kafka 'seems to wield more power in contemporary China than any other modern Western writer'. One example is the work of Can Xue, one of the most acclaimed avant-garde writers in China today. At the age of seventy, her experimental work is finally gaining wide recognition on the anglophone literary scene too: translations of her books were longlisted for the International Booker Prize twice in the last five years. Her passion for Kafka, in particular *The Castle*, is well known; an English translation of her analysis of his writing is forthcoming from Yale University Press. Even her pseudonym – 'Can Xue' means 'leftover' or 'stubborn' snow – resonates with the vast, snowy landscape of Kafka's last novel.

Polar Bear Reads Kafka

If Can Xue has played a special part in creating a space for Kafka in contemporary Chinese literature, Yoko Tawada has taken on a similar role in Japan – but in her case, the boundary between Japanese- and German-language literature has been porous in particularly distinctive ways. Let me explain what I mean by this by introducing you to one of my favourite literary responses to Kafka in the twenty-first century, which also happens to feature one of my favourite readers of Kafka. She might be a fictional character, but who could resist her? Meet the female anthropomorphic polar bear who has emigrated from Soviet Russia to West Germany and is currently working hard on improving her fluency in the German language in order to write a bestselling memoir.

For my money, Tawada – the author of *Memoirs of a Polar Bear* (2014) – is one of the most exciting writers at work today. She crafts some of her prize-winning poetry, novels, stories, plays and essays in Japanese, her mother tongue, and some in German, a language in which she developed fluency after moving to Germany at the age of twenty-two; often she produces versions of her work in both these languages, and sometimes writes texts that combine them. Tawada has won some of the most prestigious literary prizes in both Japan and Germany, including the Akutagawa Prize and the Kleist Prize. She loves a good pun, the kind of wordplay that becomes more obvious when one looks at a language as an outsider, a non-native speaker. Kafka has long played a special role in her writing. In 1998, she gave a series of influential lectures in German, titled *Metamorphoses*; in 2009, she identified Kafka as the most important German-language writer for her own work, above all his *Metamorphosis*; a year later, she creatively adapted this story as a Japanese play, *Kafka Kaikoku*.

In *Memoirs of a Polar Bear*, Tawada clearly bestows on her titular protagonist-narrator some of her own fascination as well as frustration with a literary life of an immigrant from what is called in German a 'minority background' and usually construed as ethnic difference. By making her protagonist-narrator an anthropomorphic animal, Tawada exposes, rhetorically heightens and mercilessly mocks the cultural prejudice that treats people like her as categorically different from other Germans: her protagonist belongs to a different species altogether, but at the same time she can walk, talk, read and write – in more than one language, in fact – which prompts a whole gamut of reactions from the human characters, from delight to fascination to unease. This tension comes to a head in what simply must be one of the best pieces of comic writing in the great tradition of migrant literature.

Let me set the scene. Having attempted to work her way through a grammar textbook, the polar bear returns to the bookshop where she had bought it in the hope of picking up some more study resources:

> The second time I visited, the bookseller came up to me right away, gave a dry cough and asked whether the language textbook had been helpful. 'I didn't understand the grammar, but the short story was interesting. The story of the mouse singer Josephine.' My answer made him laugh. 'The grammar is superfluous if you understood the story.'

The story from the textbook is 'Josefine, the Singer or The Mouse-People' (1924), one of Kafka's many stories featuring anthropomorphic animals. The bookseller thinks he is on safe ground; surely that cast of characters must be what attracted the polar bear to the story. He promptly picks up another volume by Kafka, explaining:

> 'Among other things, he wrote several stories from the point of view of animals.' When our eyes met, something seemed to occur to him that he found puzzling. Hurriedly he added: 'What I mean is that this literature is valuable as literature, not because it was written from a minority perspective.'

Uh-oh – he knows he is in trouble! The reader, meanwhile, can just about picture Tawada's wry smile; she knows first-hand how difficult it is for somebody pigeon-holed as a 'minority writer' to gain the same kind of recognition as 'majority writers' (who, unsurprisingly, are never labelled in this way) – to have her literature read 'as literature', rather than a factual exposé on socio-political issues facing her demographic. Kafka is one such writer; as we have seen in previous chapters, despite the profound influence that his identity had on his writing, and many attempts over the years to read his work primarily as an expression of his identity as a German-speaking Jew in Prague, this critical lens has not got in the way of a broad array of other interpretations, making Kafka into a universal classic.

The bookseller's monologue about Kafka continues: 'In fact, the main character is never an animal. During the process by which an animal is transformed into a non-animal or a human into a non-human, memory gets lost, and it's this loss that is the main character.' I can just picture this German bookseller looking expectantly at the polar bear to gauge her reaction: he has done well, has he not? Shown that he can appreciate the aesthetic payoff of the choice to write literature from a 'minority perspective'? But to her, 'his lecture was too much side salad without a main course'. I first encountered this passage when it was read out at a prize-giving ceremony for a translation award. Once we got to the bit about 'too much side salad', the audience roared with laughter, and I knew I had to get my hands on this novel.

Having playfully undercut the bookseller's pretentions as a literary theorist who can confidently explain to an animal how to read stories about animals, the polar bear goes on: 'I couldn't follow, but I didn't want him to notice. So I lowered my eyes and pretended to be having profound thoughts about the book.' Let us lower our eyes too as she picks up her new book of Kafka's stories: 'I opened the book the way you might break a loaf of peasant bread in two. My nails were too long to make it easy to flip through a book's pages. In earlier years, I'd attempted to trim them but wound up spilling a lot of blood. Now I just let them grow.'

In a pitch-perfect transition, Tawada – and her English translator, the great Susan Bernofsky – have taken me from uproarious laughter to a moment of startled silence. Suddenly we are not in a comedy, but a drama which mobilises social histories of the rise of literacy, family histories of upward social mobility, where books enter homes for the first time, both as foreign, unwieldy objects, and as portals to other lives. The image of blood spilling as the polar bear trims her fingernails to better grasp a book is shocking; the quiet defiance as she decides to let them grow out is moving. Such are the emotional and socio-cultural regions to which the German-Japanese writer takes us in her memoir of an Arctic species adapting to life among Europeans by reading Kafka. This light-touch and yet deeply resonant mix of comedy and pathos is characteristic of Kafka's works, especially – as we are about to see – of his animal stories.

The Animal Artist and Her Message

The story from the polar bear's textbook, 'Josefine, the Singer or The Mouse-People', is not only one of Kafka's many stories featuring anthropomorphic animals – it is also the very last text he wrote and published before his death, and it directly addresses the questions of what art is, what it is for and what the relationship between an artist and their audience is. It is narrated by an unnamed mouse on behalf of the titular mouse folk, one member of which – Josefine – is a singer. Her singing enthrals other mice even though they do not otherwise care for music, art or other 'things that are as remote from the rest of our life', and in fact this 'singing' is possibly just a form of 'Pfeifen' – piping, peeping, whistling or squeaking – the ordinary sound produced by mice. Here we come upon another example of Kafka's 'gleitendes Paradox' – a 'sliding', 'gliding' or 'shifting' paradox, a term coined by the influential Germanist Gerhard Neumann to describe the quality of much of Kafka's writing, its tendency to seemingly establish clear, simple facts – 'our singer is called Josefine', reads the first sentence of the story – only to question, subvert or undermine them, forcing the reader to remain vigilant and constantly course-correct: Josefine might actually not sing at all, just squeak.

But this is not the end; the paradox keeps sliding; in fact, to our narrator it seems that Josefine is not even able to squeak as well as the other mice – her voice is unusually weak! What is 'the riddle of the great effect she has' then – how come her compatriots treat her like an artist? Well, she behaves like a real diva, for one thing – but the decisive factor is that Josefine 'is someone ceremoniously presenting herself – in order to do nothing different from the usual thing'. More than one scholar has compared this idea of an everyday activity elevated to the status of performance art to Marcel Duchamp's 1917 provocative display of a urinal under the title *Fountain*. Duchamp described such pieces as 'everyday objects elevated to the dignity of a work of art by the artist's act of choice'. This is a radically modern understanding of what art is: not any specific class of objects or practices, but a social act through which somebody gets others to pay attention to something – crucially, without a call for any further action.

The mice do indeed pay attention to Josefine's art of the everyday: they sit 'mäuschenstill' when she performs – a pun that Tawada must appreciate, since the word means 'as quiet as a mouse'. But does Josefine pay attention to her folk? Another pun Kafka uses is the word 'pfeifen', to 'whistle' or 'pipe' – but the idiom 'auf etwas pfeifen', which is also deployed in the story, means 'to not give a damn about something'. Both these puns raise the question of Josefine's relationship to her folk, and vice versa. Josefine stages her impromptu performances whenever the mice suffer particular setbacks in their hard and precarious collective existence; apparently she sees herself as a protector or even saviour of her folk. But another possibility is also floated: Josefine could be trying simply to coax her compatriots into providing for her by putting on airs. Be that as it may, through her performances she creates an opportunity for the mouse folk to come together – both metaphorically and literally, as they form a thick throng before her.

In this way, it would seem that Josefine constitutes a community – but also allows for individuals to recognise themselves as individuals. Her singing 'reaches the individual almost like a message from the people' because it appears to represent 'the miserable existence of our people in the midst of the tumult of a hostile world'; it is 'freed of the fetters of daily life, and it also sets us free, for a short while'. The story does not use the word, but a nest of mice like this can be described in German by the uncountable noun 'Ungeziefer', or 'pest' – the word used in *The Metamorphosis* to refer to Gregor after his transformation. This is one of the reasons why many scholars have read 'Josefine' as a parable for the plight of the Jewish people in an anti-Semitic world. Josefine's art seems to make free individuals worthy of respect out of what others seek to humiliate as the collective 'Ungeziefer', while at the same time reclaiming the value of this community in the face of prejudice. But it is important to remember that the gravity of such a possible parabolical message is balanced out by the humour of the story, evident, for example, in the puns we just looked at. The suggestion of a serious message is clothed in gentle comedy.

As so often with Kafka, the text is also full of careful qualifiers: what we are told is only how things 'seem' or 'appear' to be. Moreover, at the end of the story Josefine takes the inexplicable decision to stop performing. The mouse folk 'continues on its way', but for her 'things are bound to go downhill': it turns out that her individual performance might not be so distinctive or central to the self-understanding of the mouse folk after all. It is difficult to resist linking Josefine's retreat into silence and the transformation of her song, or squeak, into the stuff of memory with Kafka's own plight in the last months, weeks and days of his life, losing his literal voice to the rapidly progressing tuberculosis of the throat, as well as his figurative voice as a writer. The story of Josefine comes across as deeply personal; Kafka was correcting the proofs for its publication in a book of stories on his deathbed.

But at the same time, as so often with his work, and with any great literature, Kafka's quaint tale of a singing or simply squeaking mouse, who possibly holds her folk together but perhaps does not give a damn, resonates far and wide – even with a polar bear. One of the key ideas in 'Josefine' is the possibility that an artist might transmit a key message through the great influence she exerts on her audience. But the mechanism by which this occurs remains mysterious. The story leaves several crucial questions open: can the audience know what the artist's intentions are, does the artist even have a clear intention in the first place, what is the precise source of her influence on her audience, what is the relationship between the audience and the artist, and between the audience and the art itself? These questions were on Kafka's mind as he lay dying, cognisant that these stories, about to be published, would outlive him. They are also the foundational questions of a whole branch of literary enquiry known by the name of reception theory – and of the book you are reading, of course. As we slowly near the end of our travels in search of Kafka, let us investigate one last case study of a particular group of Kafka's readers – perhaps the one that Kafka would have found the hardest to imagine or predict because, at first glance, they seem to share the least with him: feminists in present-day South Korea.

Kafka's Message Reaches Korea

Asked in an interview about the significance of Kafka for her literary formation, Yoko Tawada emphasised how well known and widely read Kafka is across East Asia. The very first translations of select short stories by Kafka appeared as early as 1933 in Japan, 1955 in Korea and 1966 in China; his works became more widely available and popular in the 1960s in Japan, 1970s in Korea and 1980s in China. Western scholars of Kafka have on occasion observed that his works have been uncommonly popular in the region. For example, in 2000 the editors of an extensive international bibliography of secondary literature on Kafka identified Japan and 'above all' Korea as the centre of Kafka's popularity in Asia and marvelled at the 'almost unbelievable' number of Korean translations. Kafka's popularity in Korea is indeed great, whether one considers the sheer number of available translations, the depth and breadth of his influence on Korean writers, the popularity and range of theatre adaptations or the volume of academic research on Kafka at Korean universities.

But in English- and German-language scholarship such observations are either relegated to highly specialist publications, or merely mentioned in passing in leading handbooks and monographs on Kafka, often with mild surprise or even naïve astonishment. This reluctance to cross borders in scholarship even remotely as readily as it occurs in cultural production itself has always irked me. Partly, I will be the first to admit, because I am myself a product of such cultural 'trans-lation', in its etymological sense of being 'brought across' a border or two, so it feels incongruous – or even intellectually dishonest – to read, write and think along national and linguistic lines, when one's own biography has been all about crossing such lines. And in this case, my personal experience is helpfully reflective of a much wider trend: the transnational nature of our cultural landscape.

But mostly I am drawn to topics like this – like Kafka in Korea – because they remind me why I wanted to become a literary scholar in the first place: on account of that exhilarating promise that somebody, sometime, somewhere could have written something so electrifying that that cultural current can still insistently hum and sing and resonate a hundred years later, on the other side of the world, on a translator's desk, in a publisher's office, on a bookseller's stand, in a reader's hand, on the pages of a new theatrical or film script, as another writer's fingers pick up a pen or hit the keyboard.

One such stimulating moment of transcultural connection took place when the first Korean translation of a text by Kafka was published by Song Suk-jae in 1955 in a literary magazine. It was two texts, in fact: 'Before the Law', which we have already looked at in Chapter Three, and 'A Message from the Emperor'. Just like 'Before the Law', 'A Message from the Emperor' was part of a longer draft which ended up being published only posthumously by Brod, under the title 'At the Building of the Great Wall of China'. But Kafka had already published this short extract in a magazine, and included it in his 1920 collection *A Country Doctor*. Here is this short piece in its entirety:

> The Emperor – so it is said – has sent to you, the solitary, the miserable subject, the infinitesimal shadow who fled the imperial sun to far and furthest parts, to you and none other, the Emperor has from his deathbed sent a message. He had the messenger kneel at his bedside and whispered the message in his ear; so important to him was it that he had it repeated in the messenger's ear once more. With a nod he confirmed that what had been said was correct. And in the presence of the entire audience for his death – all the walls that might be in their way are demolished,

and the grandees of the empire are standing in a circle on the wide, high sweep of the outer flight of steps – in the presence of all those assembled he sent the messenger on his way. The messenger has set off at once; a sturdy man, unwearying; stretching forward first one arm, then the other, he pushes his way through the crowd; if he meets with resistance, he points to his chest, which bears the sign of the sun; and he moves forward with an ease no one can match. But the crowd is so vast, their dwellings never come to an end. If open country stretched out before him, how he would fly, and soon, no doubt, you would hear the commanding sound of his fists beating upon your door. But instead, how uselessly he labours; he is still forcing his way through the chambers of the innermost palace; he will never get through them; and if he managed that, there would be nothing gained; he would have to fight his way down the stairs; and if he managed that, there would be nothing gained; the courtyards would have to be crossed; and after the courtyards, the second, outer palace; and again more stairs and more courtyards; and again a palace; and so on through the millennia; and if at last he emerged, stumbling, through the outermost gates – but that can never, never happen – the imperial city still lies before him, the centre of the world, piled high with its own refuse. No one will get through here – and certainly not with a message from the dead. – You, though, will sit at your window and conjure it up for yourself in your dreams, as evening falls.*

---

* Translation © Joyce Crick 2012. Reproduced with permission of the Licensor through PLSclear.

Of Kafka's many pieces of microfiction, this is one of the best known – and possibly my favourite. The setting is Kafka's imaginary ancient China, which, as it turns out, strangely intersects with Kafka's lived reality: he wrote these lines in 1917, soon after his own emperor's death. Franz Joseph I died in November 1916 at the age of eighty-six, after sixty-eight years on the imperial throne, up there with Louis XIV and Elizabeth II. He was succeeded by his grand-nephew, but really the days of empire were over: it would be formally dissolved at the end of the war, two years after Franz Joseph I's death.

Kafka's 'Message from the Emperor' is presented as a legend, as signalled by the 'so it is said' in the first sentence, but at the same time, it is told in the unusual second person singular, using the German pronoun 'du' – the informal 'you' – which makes it sound like secret, intimate communication between the teller and the 'solitary' or 'singular' reader. This, of course, is exactly the character of the emperor's message itself too. The whole vignette is shaped around the contrast between the intimacy of the whispered message and the vast, unbridgeable, completely and utterly overwhelming distance, the 'fernste Ferne', literally 'remotest remoteness', separating 'you' from the dying emperor. 'You' are the 'miserable subject', the 'infinitesimal shadow' to the emperor's sun.

There is the message, and then there is the messenger: 'a sturdy man, unwearying'; 'he moves forward with an ease no one can match'. At this point in the text, even a reader used to Kafka's endless withholding paradoxes would be excused for harbouring a little hope that the message might yet reach the intended recipient. But this hope is almost immediately dashed: 'the crowd is so vast, their dwellings never come to an end.' In fact, the messenger is still in the chambers of the innermost palace! The text pivots now to an overlong, painfully protracted, utterly draining single sentence, which takes up nearly a third of the whole piece and conveys the superhuman efforts of the messenger, which are in the end all in vain. This sentence in particular is strongly reminiscent of 'Before the Law', with its exhausting list of nestling conditionals, all the 'even ifs' that separate the messenger from 'you', the recipient – or 'the man from the country' from 'the Law' in the earlier parable.

After a final dash comes the conclusion: 'You, though, will sit at your window and conjure it up for yourself in your dreams, as evening falls.' And so it turns out that, even though we never find out what that momentous message is – in German, 'Botschaft' (the same word is later used with reference to Josefine's singing in the story of the mouse folk) is not just a simple 'Nachricht', information or communication, but rather 'tidings', or even 'gospel'; in the context of this story, the German word clearly implies metaphysical weight – 'you', the recipient, have the capacity to dream up what it might be. It is this surprise ending, alongside the unusual narrative voice that speaks in the second person singular, that marks a decisive departure from the hopelessness of 'Before the Law'. Both these features raise the possibility of individual agency, of an independent 'you' with dreams that are not absolutely bound by a higher law, even if they quietly unfold in its shadow.

It is this text, which began in an imaginary space between ancient China and Kafka's own crumbling empire, and thematises the impossibility of communication only to transcend it in the final sentence, that inaugurates his presence in Korean literature in 1955 – which strikes me as a fitting metaphor for the power of translation. From there, a veritable tidal wave of translations followed. Lee Yu-sun and Mok Seong-sook, two Germanists from the Korean Kafka Society, counted seventy-seven separate translations of various texts by Kafka – literary works, diaries and letters – that appeared in 127 books and ten magazines by 1989, and more and more translations after that, accounting for almost all pieces of writing ever produced by Kafka, and culminating in the complete works based on the German critical edition. Lee and Mok estimated that *The Castle* alone was translated into Korean more than thirty-seven times between 1960 and 2003.

A 'Writers' Writer'

As in many other countries, in Korea the most popular of Kafka's books has long been *The Metamorphosis*; the term 'Kafkaesque' has entered the everyday language; Kafka's early reception was heavily influenced by French Existentialism; and his writings offered a clever way to circumvent censorship and offer the Korean public a 'projection screen' for its struggle under an undemocratic, repressive political system. According to Lee and Mok, the 'inescapable scenarios in which Kafka's characters find themselves' could serve for South Korean readers as a 'path for escape from their unfreedom' during the long years of military dictatorship from 1961 to 1987.

Kafka has also long served, as Lee and Mok put it, as a 'writers' writer': a recurring source of inspiration for successive generations of Korean authors. They describe a whole host of novels and stories, almost without exception unavailable in English translation, that take their cue from Kafka. In Kim Young-hyun's *Insect* (1989), to take one example, the narrator reads Kafka's *Metamorphosis* and contrasts Gregor Samsa with his own life as a political prisoner: treated like an insect by the prison guards, he rejects what he sees as Kafka's hopelessness to preserve his own sense of humanity. In *Kafka's Marriage* (1998), Germanist Kim Jung-suk's first foray into fiction, the protagonist is an ageing bachelor obsessed with Kafka. In Kim Yeon-kyung's *Trial* (2000), the narrator falls asleep while watching Orson Welles's adaptation of Kafka's novel and has a dream in which, like Josef K., she is inexplicably arrested one day. In Koo Hyo-seo's *At Night As I Read Kafka* (2002), a novelist loses his bearings while battling an inner ear infection and, as the title has it, reading Kafka all night long: both are 'conditions', as it were, that affect the novelist's ability to hear his own voice.

In their writing on Kafka, Korean authors often register a distinct unease that emerges in encounters between an iconic classic of world literature and a contemporary writer whose own language and literary culture tend to be perceived as provincial and marginal. In 1987, for example, Oh Kyu-won wrote the following short poem, quoted here in Shyun J. Ahn's translation:

— MENU —
Charles Baudelaire 800 won
Carl Sandburg 800 won
Franz Kafka 800 won

Yves Bonnefoy 1,000 won
Erica Jong 1,000 won
Gaston Bachelard 1,200 won
Ihab Hassan 1,200 won
Jeremy Rifkin 1,200 won
Jürgen Habermas 1,200 won
Sitting by my crazy student
who wants to study poetry,
I drink
the cheapest coffee,
Franz Kafka

Out of this Korean menu of foreign – European and North American – writers and intellectuals *cum* hot drinks divided into three different price tags, Kafka is singled out as 'the cheapest coffee', drunk by a poet whose disciple is 'crazy'. Crazy because, presumably, they are both broke and literature – like coffee – is an imported luxury. The year 1987 was a breakthrough for South Korea: about to focus the attention of the whole world during the 1988 Summer Olympics in Seoul, following years of such unprecedented economic growth pursued by a succession of authoritarian rulers that it was dubbed 'the miracle on the Han River' after the river flowing across Seoul, a string of protests shook the country, leading to the inauguration of the country's first ever democratically elected president. Under such circumstances, the poet seems to ask, how can one afford – both literally and figuratively – to write poetry? Except that all this is communicated to us in a poem, of all things, one whose highly economical, sharp and tight form playfully concedes the need to economise, while also implying that literary expression is a necessity: a basic good rather than luxury. It is only fitting that the patron saint of this piece is Kafka – of all the writers listed on the menu, the least verbose, the master of the micro-form, but also the one who proclaimed that he lived to write – that writing was for him the condition of living.

Decades later, in Gu Byeong-mo's 2013 novel *The Old Woman with the Knife*, the protagonist and first-person narrator works as a contract killer in a company that uses insect extermination as a front. Thinking about her targets, she muses: 'You don't need some Kafkaesque interpretation of how a person, gradually over a long period of time, or sometimes suddenly overnight, becomes vermin.' The reference to Kafka is dropped in passing, but nevertheless strongly resonates with the novel's broader theme and plot. What these two superficially simple but in fact complex and telling examples show is that the act of choosing Kafka as an intertext – or playfully refusing to do so ('You don't need some Kafkaesque interpretation', Gu's narrator insists) – becomes an active, creative and reflective act of transcultural connection, rather than an instance of passive reception.

While neither the novels discussed by Lee and Mok nor Oh's poetry are well known in the English-speaking world, *The Old Woman with the Knife* appeared in English in 2022 bearing endorsements from bestselling writers like Paula Hawkins (*The Girl on the Train*) and Luke Jennings (*Codename Villanelle*) and was widely reviewed, including in the *London Review of Books*, *Financial Times* and *The New York Times*. Part of the reason for its success is its genre: thriller rather than literary fiction, let alone poetry. But Korean literary fiction has been making inroads into the

English-language market too, and strikingly often Kafka has been in the picture, in one way or another.

Kafkaesque Korean Wave?

Numerous recently translated contemporary Korean novels and short-story collections – especially written by women – have been introduced to English readers as 'Kafkaesque', whether by publishers, reviewers or prize committees. The most successful example is *The Vegetarian* by Han Kang, the winner of the 2016 Man Booker International Prize along-side translator Deborah Smith, but recently translated books by Bae Suah, Cho Nam-joo, Yun Ko-eun, Pyun Hye-young, Kim Young-ha, Lee Ki-ho, Ch'oe In-ho and Jung Young-moon, among others, have also been compared to Kafka's works or characterised as 'Kafkaesque'.

The more such books I came across, the more intrigued I became. Is Kafka a secret agent of the 'Korean wave', I wondered? In case you have not come across this term before, it refers to 'the rise of international interest in South Korea and its popular culture which took place in the late twentieth and twenty-first centuries', according to the *Oxford English Dictionary*, which in 2021 added this term – alongside twenty-five others – in a self-described 'K-update', itself a manifestation of the Korean wave.

Since the 1990s, South Korea's government has relentlessly pursued an agenda, in scholar Jenny Wang Medina's words, 'to redefine its cultural identity through direct investment into cultural industries'. This agenda was further expanded in the wake of the Asian financial crisis of 1997 to make culture a cornerstone of the national economy in a globalised world. This 'culture' or – in a Konglish (Korean-English) neologism coined by the state administration in the 2000s – 'munhwa *kontencheu*', 'cultural *content*' (my italics), initially referred to mass-marketed products like pop music and TV series. But what we might think of as 'highbrow' or 'prestigious' literature and cinema did not remain untouched by this process either. In 1996, the Korean Literature Translation Fund was set up by the government. Now known as the Literature Translation Institute of Korea, it financially supports the publication of a staggering proportion of Korean novels in English, as well as numerous other languages. Its annual budget in 2021 exceeded ₩12 billion (£7 million). Its stated mission is the 'development and globalization of Korean literature'; its 2021 annual report juggles tidal metaphors, proposing to 'bring a fresh current to world literature by stirring up a wave of Korean literature' and thus 'expand the Korean wave driven by K-pop and K-drama into the realm of literature to make it deeper and more diverse'. This is not just a government agenda: many private companies in Korea now have cultural foundations that support similar endeavours too.

I must have been very susceptible to these concerted efforts to promote Korean culture abroad, beyond K-pop and K-drama, from early on, even if – or perhaps precisely because – initially I had little understanding of the tidal wave that hit me. In 2010, a school friend takes me to an arthouse screening of Park Chan-wook's thriller *Oldboy* (2003). In its electrifying opening scenes, we meet Oh Dae-su, a man who has been imprisoned for fifteen years without knowing the identity or motivation of his captor. Echoes of Josef K. from *The Trial* are clear: Park lists Kafka as one of the main sources of inspiration for his cinematic art. I am not aware of this at the time, but *Oldboy* is the first Korean film to achieve major international success. It wins the Grand Prix at Cannes and becomes a critically acclaimed box-office hit around the world. I start catching up on Park's earlier films, following his now firmly international career, and watch other Korean films, of which more and more are being screened in my local cinema, and becoming available on screening platforms. I also pick up *Please Look After Mom* (2008), which appears in translation in 2011 and becomes the biggest international publishing success for a Korean novel at that point. Its author, Kyung-Sook Shin, lists Kafka as the novelist she most admires. Then Han Kang's supposedly 'Kafkaesque' *Vegetarian* wins the Man Booker International Prize: I read it; I like it – more Korean literature is becoming available in translation. I am hooked.

When I finally start learning Korean in 2017, one of the first texts our class painstakingly inches our way through, once we have enough grammar and vocabulary to start reading authentic material, is Hwang Sun-won's 'Rain Shower', a short story from 1952 so central to the national psyche that it has its own museum near Seoul. The other text we slowly work our way through that year is a speech titled 'The Country's Future Depends on the Cultural Content Industry' given in 2014 by the CEO of one of the big South Korean entertainment and mass-media companies, a subsidiary of the largest of all Korean conglomerates, known as 'chaebols', controlled by the family who also owns Samsung. This pairing of texts might come across as random, the way a friend of mine was asked in an intermediate German class to read a text about recycling swiftly followed by one on anti-Nazi resistance during the Second World War. Except that nothing is random about such selections: whether intentionally or not, they communicate what a given culture sees as central to its own self-understanding. In the case of South Korea, it is culture – but also the political support given to this culture with a hope – no, goal, or even better, detailed plan – of making it go global.

Which it does: even if not as fantastically profitable as K-pop and K-drama, over the last decade Korean literature – sometimes even dubbed 'K-lit', not least by the South Korean Ministry of Culture, Sports and Tourism – has been making steady inroads into other countries around the world too. As Wang Medina explains, the new, internationally successful canon of Korean literature in translation emerged out of a 'collaboration of the state, corporate interests, and the literary establishment that once strongly opposed them'. In 2014, for example, Korea was the 'market focus' at the London Book Fair. One of the ten Korean authors promoted at the event was Han Kang, who at that point had been publishing in Korean for some twenty years, but whose work was yet to appear in English. Smith's translation of Han's *The Vegetarian* came out the following year, in which, according to a Nielsen BookScan report, the combined sales of Korean books in the UK exceeded 10,000 copies – up from just 88 in 2001. The subsequent award of the Man Booker International Prize to *The Vegetarian* marked the first time that a global literary award of this stature went to a Korean book, and cemented the 'Korean wave' in literature.

Now, to come back to my opening question: how much do the books translated as part of the Korean wave and dubbed 'Kafkaesque' in fact have to do with Kafka? In some, as we shall see later in this chapter, Kafka is absolutely central. In others, there are no explicit allusions to Kafka at all, but they attract comparisons to his work anyway – and examining the reasons why offers valuable clues both to the source of Kafka's enduring popularity and to the workings of the global literary market.

Kafka the Feminist

One of the biggest success stories in Korean publishing of the last decade is a case in point. Cho Nam-joo's novel *Kim Jiyoung, Born 1982* (2016), a dispassionate chronicle of the casual sexism experienced by an ordinary Korean woman in the course of her everyday life, resulting in a nervous breakdown, sold more than a million copies in South Korea. When Jamie Chang's English translation came out in 2020, it was widely reviewed, including in *The New York Times*, where Euny Hong, a prominent Korean-American journalist and writer, compared Cho's narrative voice to that of Kafka's in *The Metamorphosis*, and Kim Jiyoung to Gregor Samsa. Like him, Hong writes, she 'feels so overwhelmed by social expectations that there is no room for her in her own body; her only option is to become something – or someone – else'. Hong likes that a key term in the novel, the insult thrown at Kim Jiyoung that precipitates her breakdown, is translated as 'mum-roach' in English – precisely because it makes her think of Kafka's *Metamorphosis*.

This is not an isolated example: Kafka keeps popping up in contemporary Korean literature written by women, or discussions thereof, and curiously often these references serve to express a particularly feminist concern about the social roles played by women in South Korean society. Novels like *Kim Jiyoung, Born 1982* capture, denounce and mobilise against gender inequality, which is damaging women's careers and personal lives, with a knock-on effect on the entire society. In 2021, it was reported that South Korea 'has the highest wage gap among the OECD members: Korean women are paid a third less on average than their male counterparts'. In 2022, the country's fertility rate hit a new record low – it is now the only country in the world where it is below one.

Kafka's own views on women's rights do not seem to play much of a role here. He was doubtlessly beholden to many sexist stereotypes of his day; female characters in his works are often presented as possessing an overwhelming, animalistic physicality and sexual force. At the same time, he developed close, intellectual friendships with several women, including his youngest sister, Ottla, whose education and attempts at an independent career in the field of agricultural management he passionately encouraged and supported. But it is not the nuances of Kafka's real-life relationships with women that inform his prominent position in the production and reception of feminist literature in contemporary Korea, but rather his startlingly evocative literary visions of psychological alienation and bodily abjection, which in his writing affect male protagonists, like Gregor Samsa from *The Metamorphosis*, and yet – as it turns out – can be translated and adapted to express feminist concerns with astonishing force.

Yeong-hye, the protagonist of Han Kang's runaway international success *The Vegetarian*, refuses to fulfil the expectations traditionally placed on Korean women. Seemingly on a whim, one day she stops eating meat – or rather all animal products; the Korean title could in fact be translated as *The Vegan*. This decision triggers an avalanche of other changes in her behaviour, and consequently in the lives of her entire family. As the novel progresses, the central question that emerges is what the endpoint of such a transformation might be. Admitted into a psychiatric institution, Yeong-hye stops taking in any food, and instead expresses a desire to turn into a tree. We rarely gain direct access to her thoughts, though: the first part of the novel – initially conceived as a series of three interconnected novellas – is narrated by her obnoxious husband, while the second and third adopt the outside perspectives of her brother-in-law and her sister, respectively.

The Vegetarian was described as 'Kafkaesque' by its US publisher Hogarth; Boyd Tonkin, the chair of the judging panel for the Man Booker International Prize, commented that he was 'thinking of Kafka' while reading Han's novel. But while both for Han's American publicists and the Booker judges Kafka and the Kafkaesque formed just one among many descriptors and points of comparison, elsewhere they came to dominate the entire presentation of Han's novel. The reviewer for *The New York Times* begins by comparing *The Vegetarian* to a few other texts, before asking: 'Ultimately, though, how could we not go back to Kafka?' When featured on Oprah Winfrey's hugely influential website, the novel was described by Dotun Akintoye thus: 'Indebted to Kafka, this story of a South Korean woman's radical transformation, which begins after she forsakes meat, will have you reading with your hand over your mouth in shock.' In a feat of compression, Lonely Planet's guidebook to Seoul represents *all* of contemporary Korean literature by just two novels: 'Kim Young-ha's *I Have the Right to Destroy Myself* (2007), which delves into alienation in contemporary Seoul, and *The Vegetarian* (2015) by Han Kang, a dark and disturbing Kafkaesque account of a woman's fantasy to turn into a tree.' Kim Young-ha is another writer who has been compared to, but has also often spoken about his admiration for Kafka – including in a viral TED Talk.

There is a thin line between Kafka's name – or brand – helping Korean writers reach new audiences abroad and hindering a deeper engagement with Korean literature in its own right. Asked about the connection to Kafka in an interview emphatically titled 'Korea's Kafka?', Han explained that as soon as her story began circulating in Korea, some readers compared it to Kafka's *Metamorphosis*, and added: 'Of course I read Kafka when I was a teenager like everyone else, and I think Kafka has become part of this world.' While not a 'direct influence', Kafka was one of the sources that 'just lived inside me', she said. Other sources Han listed in the interview are a traditional Korean story from the Joseon Dynasty, and Yi Sang – a landmark modernist, whose works themselves have sometimes been compared to Kafka's writing. But these references are lost on most readers outside of Korea. For many such readers, Han's novel has functioned less as a gateway to the long, rich tradition of Korean literature, and more – as one scholar observed – as a 'grandchild' of European modernism, embodied above all by Kafka.

And yet it is also possible to tell a more positive story about this transcultural encounter, a story of a reciprocal boost, a win–win situation for all the books and authors involved. First of all, many Korean writers clearly do read and find inspiration in Kafka's works. Comparisons to

Kafka also helped *The Vegetarian* gain international renown, and, as Sooyun Yum from the Literature Translation Institute of Korea explains, despite considerable critical success at home, it only became a 'nationwide bestseller' in Korea after it won the Man Booker International Prize. The success of *The Vegetarian* then opened the door for more contemporary Korean books, especially by women, and especially about feminist concerns, to be translated, published and read more widely. And it seems, at least anecdotally, that the Kafka brand can really help make other books a publishing success. Some years ago, Takako Fujita from the University of Tokyo reported a 'Kafka legend' circulating in the Japanese publishing industry: 'If you want to make a new release a bestseller, you should refer to Kafka in the title or the content, and it might be enough to just use the word "Kafka".' Meanwhile, Merriam-Webster reported in the 'Trend Watch' section on its website that searches for 'Kafkaesque' in the online dictionary 'spiked dramatically' the day Han's and Smith's prize was announced. It is not just that Kafka prompted an interest in *The Vegetarian*, then, but *The Vegetarian* helped boost an interest in Kafka too.

Han's novel has been compared not only to *The Metamorphosis*, but also to Kafka's later story 'A Hunger Artist' (1922), in which a man performatively fasts while on display in a cage. Kafka himself was vegetarian – his typical evening meal, he reported to Felice Bauer in 1912, might include yogurt, pumpernickel, butter, chestnuts, dates, figs, grapes, almonds, raisins, pumpkin, bananas, apples, pears or oranges. No meat dishes, favoured by his father, were involved. While no character in Kafka's works is vegetarian, thanks to Han we now have an unforgettable vegetarian character who inhabits the same literary universe as Kafka and his literary creations.

Milena, Milena, Ecstatic

Unlike in *Kim Jiyoung, Born 1982* and *The Vegetarian*, motifs from Kafka's work appear directly and centrally in books by Bae Suah, who has also translated a selection of Kafka's works into Korean in a collection called *Dream*. Her 2003 novel, *The Essayist's Desk* (published in English as *A Greater Music*), is set in Germany, and its Korean appeared to some readers as though it had been translated from German, which made for a controversial reception among Korean literati. Its Korean protagonist recalls reading Kafka's *Castle* during an interminable, lonely winter in Germany, while attempting to learn German. Even more pointedly, Bae's 2016 novella *Milena, Milena, Ecstatic* is about a man who cannot stop reading Kafka's letters to his lover and translator, Milena Jesenská – quite literally: whenever he reaches for any book, what ends up in his hand is a copy of the letters. Here the omnipresence of Kafka becomes a theme in its own right, and is also given a feminist spin.

Like Han, Bae is now in her fifties; both published their first works in 1993; both were brought into international prominence by Deborah Smith's translations in the last ten years; and in both cases these translations were financed by one of the two biggest grant-making bodies that support Korean writers and translators: the Literature Translation Institute of Korea, a government agency, and the Daesan Foundation, a private cultural institution set up by the founder of the chaebol Kyobo Life Insurance Co., Ltd.

Transnational connections are at the centre of the vision for a Korean culture with a global reach and prestige supported by such cultural foundations. Wang Medina quotes the concluding remarks in President Kim Young-sam's flagship address of 1995 on the 'Specific Steps to Promote Globalisation': 'Our culture and our ways of thought and behaviour must also be made fitting for globalisation. We must rediscover the intrinsic richness of our traditional culture and blend it with global culture. We must march into the world with an open mind and have both pride in our own culture and respect for that of others.' *Milena, Milena, Ecstatic* seems to encapsulate this vision, albeit in a rather Kafkaesque way. This, I think, is the best place to begin to grasp what it is that Kafka might be doing for – or to – contemporary feminist literature in Korea.

Even just holding a copy of the English translation of *Milena, Milena, Ecstatic* published in 2019 makes me feel like I have my finger on the pulse of world literature: the thin chapbook has a cool geometric cover design with bold colour blocks and much typographic experimentation, not least in the title, author and the name of the series, which are written out in both Latin and Korean scripts. All the paratextual information screams *hip*: the series 'showcases the work of some of the most exciting writers working in Korean today' – almost all women – and is a 'unique collaboration between an international group of independent creative practitioners'; the project is supported by the National Centre for Writing affiliated with the University of East Anglia, known for nurturing exciting new voices in English literature; translator Deborah Smith 'has recently moved to Seoul, where she aims to commission and collaborate on writing projects on translation and decolonisation, and literature as a social and activist practice'. And at the centre of this contemporary, hip, cool, creative, international, feminist enterprise: our old friend, Franz Kafka.

Milena, Milena, Ecstatic is the story of Hom Yun, a budding Korean director, who – much to his surprise – has just received a grant for his independent, obscure documentary about a woman looking for her mother among the Scythian graves of Central Asia. The grant comes from a Korean cultural foundation run by a large private company, subtly reminding us of the workings of the country's 'cultural content industry'. Like Hom Yun's film, the English translation of *Milena, Milena, Ecstatic* was also financially supported by a cultural foundation – in this case, the Literature Translation Institute of Korea.

But on the day Hom Yun is to sign the contract with the foundation, a series of mysterious events disrupts the highly regulated flow of his daily life. The central mysterious event concerns a book – appropriately, since 'what Hom Yun loves most is reading a book while immersed in lukewarm water'. He also enjoys reading in many other circumstances, and carefully chooses different authors and genres to suit the occasion. Almost all of them are Western classics: Dante, Shakespeare, Pinter, Ionesco, Beckett, Whitman, Eliot. But on this particular day, 'with his body immersed in the water, he picks up the topmost book from the small pile balanced on the edge of the tub' only to discover that he does not recognise this book at all; he does not know how it even made it into his house. The book is *Letters to Milena*.

Like many of his contemporaries, Kafka left behind copious correspondence: letters to family members, friends, acquaintances, editors, colleagues, institutions – and lovers. He had serious relationships with four women; he got engaged to two of them – twice to one! – and broke off all three engagements. Sizeable collections of letters to two of these women have survived: Felice Bauer and Milena Jesenská. Published as *Letters to Felice* and *Letters to Milena*, they have much exercised readers' imaginations since they first appeared in the 1950s and 1960s. This fascination is in fact so widespread that it has now gone mainstream: in February 2023, the *Daily Mail* ran a headline that read: 'He Is My Bare Minimum: Franz Kafka Becomes an Unlikely Heartthrob on TikTok'. A wave of teenage female readers has been posting short videos about Kafka, especially his letters to Jesenská, which supposedly set an enviable standard for twenty-first-century courtship.

There are indeed many moving and intimate passages in Kafka's letters to Bauer and Jesenská, which suggest that he respected and appreciated the two women in ways that were not a given at the time. For example, in both cases he admired and valued their professional activities. Both women had interesting, successful careers: Bauer was a marketer for a cutting-edge company producing gramophones and dictation machines known as parlographs, and Jesenská was a journalist and translator. In fact, she produced the first translation of a text by Kafka into any language: 'The Stoker', the first chapter of the unfinished novel *The Man who Disappeared*, which Kafka had published as a standalone story in 1913. Jesenská's Czech translation was published in 1920.

But other passages in Kafka's letters come across as insensitive, self-centred or possessive. I always feel uncomfortable reading these letters, partly because they were clearly never intended for publication so reading them feels invasive and voyeuristic on some level, but also because of how the book editions of these letters frame the women. The titles only use their first names, which is often reproduced in scholarship: Kafka is always Kafka, whereas Bauer and Jesenská are usually Felice and Milena. This makes it too easy to overlook the fact that, just like Kafka himself, these women were fully fledged individuals with their own lives, interests and opinions, including on their relationships with him.

This is magnified by the fact that their responses to Kafka's letters are almost entirely unknown. While Kafka does not appear to have held on to the correspondence he received, except for some letters from Brod, the two women meticulously collected his letters and ensured their survival. Bauer kept almost all of the more than five hundred letters Kafka had sent her, brought them with her to the US, where she emigrated with her husband in the 1930s, and only sold them in 1956 for a relatively modest sum of $8,000 to Kafka's American publisher when, in her old age, she ran into financial difficulties. (Twenty years later they would be sold again – this time to an anonymous buyer, for $605,000.) Meanwhile, Jesenská entrusted Kafka's letters to their common friend and prominent literary editor, Willy Haas, upon the Nazi occupation of Prague in 1939. Since she was herself a writer, many of her other writings have survived; some are available in English or German translation, but none has generated nearly as much interest as *Letters to Milena*.

Bae's novella depicts this fixation on Jesenská as a romantic interest of Kafka, at the expense of Jesenská as a real-life woman and writer in her own right, reaching gargantuan proportions. She is not just 'Milena' here, but – as the title has it – 'Milena, Milena, Ecstatic'. A variation on this phrase is also what Hom Yun notices first when he opens up the book of Kafka's letters:

> Hom Yun examines the inside cover. There, someone has written a sentence in German, in pencil. Stiff and crooked, as though the writer were not familiar with the German alphabet and had simply copied out the words, the handwriting scattered clumsily and slanted irregularly and in individual strokes that did not join up with each other.

> 'Ecstatic Milena'

> There are no markings other than that single sentence, which he absolutely had not written himself. This means that this book is not Hom Yun's.

'Hwangholhan', the Korean word that Smith translates as 'ecstatic' across the novella, including in its title, can also mean 'magnificent', 'splendid', 'brilliant'; it can describe both the thing which causes ecstasy and the person who experiences it. What is 'hwangholhan' in the story is not just Milena, but also the energy that Kafka's letters to her generate or unleash in Hom Yun's life, which up until that point had been exceedingly orderly and governed by fixed routines, presented to us in the opening pages of the story.

A big part in the thrilling irregularity that enters Hom Yun's life is played by the unexpected incursion of the German language into his life and reading. The adjective describing

Milena is transmitted to us in the text as the Korean 'hwang-holhan', but at the same time we are informed that what it in fact conveys is a German word. This quality is what literary scholar Rebecca Walkowitz calls 'born translated': at the centre of Bae's Korean text is a phrase translated from German, but this German original does not in fact exist. In this way, Bae – one of Kafka's Korean translators – writes about Jesenská – Kafka's first translator into any language – by means of an imagined translation. Even though the German language is not directly reproduced in the novella, its spectre enters the world of Bae's story: it is unfamiliar, foreign, unread – but utterly fascinating.

Korean-Mongolian-German-Czech

But while German, the primary language of Kafka's letters to Jesenská, does not appear in the text and is instead rendered in Korean, Jesenská's Czech does resurface – quoted back to her by Kafka. This is remarkable: Bae finds an ingenious way of transmitting the earlier translator's voice in spite of her letters having been lost. Two short excerpts from Kafka's letters are quoted in *Milena, Milena, Ecstatic*, and they are among the most brilliant passages from the three hundred pages of his letters to Jesenská, a lot of which I find, quite frankly, insufferable. The first quotation is from a letter written in Prague, on 14 July 1920, a Wednesday, and it begins with another quotation – from Jesenská's letter sent from Vienna:

You write: 'Ano máš pravdu, mám ho ráda. Ale F., i tebe mám ráda.' ['Yes, you are right, I do love him. But F., I also love you.'] – I am reading this sentence very exactly, every word, pausing in particular at the 'i' ['and'], it is all correct, You wouldn't be Milena if it weren't correct and what would I be if You weren't and it's also better that You write it in Vienna than if You said it in Prague, all this I perfectly understand, maybe better than You and yet, out of some weakness I can't get over the sentence, it is an endless reading and in the end I write it down here one more time, so that You see it as well and so that we read it together, temple to temple. (Your hair against my temple.)

An earlier letter is quoted later on in *Milena, Milena, Ecstatic*, written in Prague on Sunday 4 July, the first one Kafka writes to Jesenská after they meet in person for the first time and spend four days in Vienna (they will only spend one more day together, later that summer, in Gmünd on the border between Austria and Czechoslovakia, where, as Kafka explains to Jesenská in another letter, the train station is Czech, but the town itself Austrian). Hom Yun takes a book out of his pocket in a café, but instead of the Beckett play he was expecting to see the book turns out to be *Letters to Milena* again:

Today Milena, Milena, Milena – I can't write anything else. But I will. So today Milena just in haste, exhaustion, not-being-there (the last will be true tomorrow too) . . . Milena! (Spoken into your left ear, while you are lying on the pitiful bed in a deep sleep of good provenance and slowly unknowingly turning from right to left toward my mouth.)

This is linguistic ecstasy: not one, not two, but three languages are at play – Korean, German and Czech – and by the time this text reaches an English reader, four. These are densely metafictional passages about writing and reading and speaking, and the attendant organs – faces, ears, mouths, tongues. This is writing in bed, not at a desk, hyper-focused on individual sentences ('Ano máš pravdu, mám ho ráda. Ale F., i tebe mám ráda.'), single words ('i', 'Milena'), even a sole letter, a sound, that 'i' which means 'and', 'too' but also constitutes the accented vowel in Milena's name, as Franz (or Frank, as Milena used to call him) observes in another letter.

Interacting with this linguistic ecstasy seems to undo something in Hom Yun and prompts a disconcerting vision: 'One morning, he may get up and find that he no longer recognizes his face . . . like a salesman discovering that he has metamorphosed into an insect'. The allusion to the opening sentence of Kafka's *Metamorphosis* is precise and unmistakeable here. And the theme of metamorphosis, or transformation, becomes the guiding one in the story: when that day comes for Hom Yun, it will make a profound truth 'tangible' to him for the first time: 'All the world's transformation and unfamiliarity are truly as shocking as literature insists.' The literature in question being perhaps less generic than the phrasing suggests: it is Kafka's *Metamorphosis*. The Korean word for 'transformation' used here is 'byeonsin', also the title of the Korean translation of Kafka's famous story.

The strange tale of Hom Yun keeps twisting and turning. He runs into the secretary from the cultural foundation which has awarded his grant, and she offers to become his filming assistant on the spot; she would be 'ecstatic' to work for him, she says. Hom Yun's copy of *Letters to Milena* slips out of his pocket and the woman examines it closely, but 'she doesn't know how to read a foreign language' or 'who Milena is'. In fact, she isn't sure of who she *herself* is. 'I'm not Milena. And if I am, I don't know it. No one does.' In this story of transformation, of shifting identities, foreign tongues and mislaid books, nothing is clear – except for one thing: the centrality of Franz Kafka, but cast here as a prism through which we can catch a glimpse of Milena Jesenská, rather than – as is often the case – the other way round.

Jesenská shares a lot with female protagonists in Bae's other works. She decided to marry Ernst Pollak, a Jewish intellectual; her father opposed the marriage and had her committed to a psychiatric institution – the diagnosis was 'pathological deficiency of moral concepts and feelings' – but ultimately she prevailed and moved with Pollak from Prague to Vienna. But the marriage was not happy; there were also financial troubles. She taught Czech, wrote, translated, had an affair with Kafka, took drugs. Later, during the Second World War, she worked in the underground to help those persecuted by the Nazis. She was arrested in 1939 and died in the Ravensbrück concentration camp on 17 May 1944.

Jesenská's life story resonates with Bae's characterisation of women who fascinate her and whom she puts at the centre of her plots:

They are women who refuse or cannot have their own place in traditional society. I love such women. Women who cannot be guaranteed social status through marriage, or women who refuse to marry in order to obtain it; women who do not suppress themselves for the sake of their parents or siblings; women who, as a result of their independent personalities, are lonely and financially precarious. Women who go their own way in accordance with their own stubbornness, and who are not afraid to do so. I am very interested in such lives.

For Bae, a prime example is shaman women. Shamanism is Korea's traditional native religion, still practised today – almost exclusively by women. Its social status is controversial, though: Bae explains that the religion and its practitioners have been 'pushed to the fringes of society over the course of the country's modernisation'. Meanwhile, in Central Asia shamanism is still widespread, and shamans – both men and women – are seen as 'intellectuals and healers . . . musicians and poets', Bae points out. This is where Hom Yun's experimental documentary is to be set, on which the alter ego of Kafka's 'Milena' from the cultural foundation wants to assist.

Bae herself had travelled to the Altai in Mongolia with a German-speaking group of European tourists; there she met Galsan Tschinag, a Mongolian shaman who became a prize-winning German-language writer, having studied German literature in East Germany in the 1960s. The journey to the Altai was a formative experience for Bae, traces of which are visible in many of her books. But this experience was channelled for her through the German language and literature: a deeply transcultural encounter. This is reflected in *Milena, Milena, Ecstatic*, a novella that revolves around a transcultural core, Korean-Mongolian-German-Czech, with Kafka and Jesenská as its spiritual guides. It is as though Bae responded to President Kim's call to 'rediscover the intrinsic richness of our traditional culture and blend it with global culture', although perhaps not quite in the way he expected. Across her oeuvre, she searches for the spiritual roots of Korean shamanism in Mongolia and interweaves them with the writings of Franz Kafka, that icon of global culture. But in *Milena, Milena, Ecstatic* the centre that holds it all is Jesenská, a woman who refused to comply with expectations.

You might think that by now we have strayed too far from Kafka's narrowly circumscribed life in early twentieth-century Prague, too far from the letter of his manuscripts, filled with his distinctive, curving handwriting and safely stored in an Oxford library. But I disagree. Kafka's imagination and creativity were rooted in his Central European universe, but always reached outwards, beyond established norms and conventions, in search of difference and complexity. Kafka lives on because he continues to be adopted and adapted by his readers around the world, especially Bae, whose fresh and exciting, multilingual, norm-busting writing is rooted in a close reading and translation of Kafka's works, who quite literally learnt German through the medium of his German, and let it infuse her Korean. I celebrate the fact that in Seoul Kafka can become a feminist ally, or be put into conversation with Mongolian shamans.

And now, if you will excuse me, I will pack my laptop away into the Kafka-emblazoned tote bag I got at a stall at my local weekly market in Oxford – the biggest bestseller, the owner of the stall assures me – and go practise my Korean by reading *The Metamorphosis* once more, this time in a Korean translation. I wonder what this transformation will be like.

CODA

Kafka in the Cloud

Mark Coeckelbergh, philosopher of media and technology, begins his new book *The Political Philosophy of AI* with a section titled '"I guess the computer got it wrong": Josef K. in the 21st century'. He quotes the opening sentence of Kafka's *Trial* and discusses it briefly, before pivoting to the recent real-life story of an African American man who was arrested in his home despite having not done anything wrong; it eventually turned out that his arrest was 'based on a flawed match from a facial recognition algorithm' known to produce false positives, especially when analysing faces of Black people. Coeckelbergh concludes: 'In the 21st-century United States, Josef K. is black and is falsely accused by an algorithm, without explanation.' And Kafka, one might add, is a prominent critic of artificial intelligence.

For Coeckelbergh is far from being alone in invoking Kafka to alert us to the dangers of AI. In *Life 3.0: Being Human in the Age of Artificial Intelligence* (2017), Max Tegmark summed up the hopes but also fears of the world's leading AI researchers, of which he is one: 'We might create societies that flourish like never before, on Earth and perhaps beyond, or a Kafkaesque global surveillance state so powerful that it could never be toppled.' Two years later, in an article titled 'To Save Us from a Kafkaesque Future, We Must Democratise AI', Stephen Cave, Director of the Leverhulme Centre for the Future of Intelligence at the University of Cambridge, posited a 'direct link between the trials of Josef K. and the ethical and political questions raised by artificial intelligence' due to the origin of both in uncontrollable, self-sufficient, nightmarish systems of bureaucracy, and quipped: 'Josef K. would immediately recognise the "computer says no" culture of our time.' His article concludes: 'Those who have historically been failed by systems of power, such as Kafka – a German-speaking Jew living in Prague – have always been particularly well-placed to recognise their opacity, arbitrariness and unaccountability.'

But it is misleading to claim that Kafka was 'failed by systems of power'. In fact he belonged to a small bureaucratic elite. While indeed a member of an ethnic and religious minority, even after Czech nationalists gained the upper hand after the breakdown of the Habsburg Empire Kafka was allowed to keep his senior civil-servant job at the Workers' Accident Insurance Institute for the Kingdom of Bohemia. There he mediated between the letter of the law, the interests of his institution, companies with their workplace accident-prevention policies and individual workers who were harmed in such accidents. Kafka was *both* a cog in the bureaucratic machinery *and* its subject, which can remind us that there is no neat separation between the actions of individuals and the system in which they live. We are not simply subject to the power of the algorithm, but part of a feedback loop that produces and refines it.

And Kafka is too. In 2021, writer Stephen Marche reported in the *New Yorker* on his experiments with Sudowrite, an application that uses GPT-3 – a form of artificial intelligence capable of performing intellectual tasks that until recently required humans, such as translation, writing and coding. 'GPT' stands for 'Generative Pre-trained Transformer', a large language model which was trained to spot patterns in texts available on the Internet and in this way learnt to write convincing prose in more than fifty languages, as well as to code, tweet and rhyme.

Marche speculates that publishers will soon start using AI to complete unfinished novels by famous authors. Kafka seems like a prime candidate, the ever-tormented writer who could not bring any of his novels to a close, and in his diary note about the writing of *The Judgement* complained: 'The confirmed conviction that with my novel writing I am in disgraceful lowlands of writing. Only in this way can writing be done, only with such cohesion, with such complete opening of the body and the soul.' What Kafka seems to decry here is a lack of the sheer computational power to write a whole novel in one go, to download all the thoughts, images, vague premonitions, associations, haunting turns of phrases into a written piece without the drawn-out and exhausting task of churning out words one by one. With his curiosity about modern technologies, would Kafka not have liked to try out ChatGPT for himself? I think he would have, and probably would have given us the most evocative description of its uncanny effect to boot.

Marche has not prompted GPT-3 to finish any of Kafka's unfinished novels, though; he has done something else. I read with interest how he inputted the opening of *The Metamorphosis* into the software and prompted it to offer a continuation:

As soon as Gregor was alone, he began to feel ill. Turning around was an effort. Even breathing was an effort. A thin stream of blood trickled from his flank down his fuzzy belly. He wanted to crawl away from it, but there was no place to go. He lay still on the spot where he had come to rest just in order to get his breath back and to stop the bleeding. 'I'm in a bad way,' said Gregor. It had never occurred to him before that he could really become ill. He had seen sick animals – a dove once in a while, which had fallen out of the nestling into the gutter and could not fly any more, or the weak infants of the woman next door who had to be picked up with the tongs and thrown into the dustbin, or the bugs his father used to bring to him when he was still a young boy and which he had liked so much.

I am rather taken by this description of sick animals, not so much because it sounds like something Kafka could have written, but because it seems like GPT-3 is picking up – foreshadowing even – key motifs from the story. It is not just about the bugs, and their connection to the father, but Gregor himself will be thrown into the dustbin by the end of the story, and the detail of being picked up with the tongs adds an appealing sense of precision – although the weak infants add a hair-raising tinge, more *Macbeth* than Kafka.

Marche also tried feeding the whole of *The Metamorphosis* into the software, upon which it produced, as he calls it, an 'extension':

When Mr. Samsa thought about moving house and how they could all pull their way up again, he couldn't suppress a shiver running down his spine – and this shiver ran down the spine of all three of them, he could see, as if they were collectively possessed and trembling all over with some sort of fever. It was more like a convulsion than a shiver. Then they calmed down, quite exhausted. Mr. Samsa thought: 'If we continue like this we'll soon be having a charwoman in our family. First thing tomorrow I'll make inquiries about suitable flats.' And then he looked up: the two women were gazing ahead and did not see that he was looking at them. All of a sudden Grete burst out laughing. 'What's that for?' asked her father. 'Well, just because,' replied Grete. And Mr. Samsa did not insist.

I find this 'extension' intriguing, in both what it gets right about Kafka's plot and style, and what it does not. 'It was more like a convulsion than a shiver', for example, is in one way a classic Kafka move – something that seems like one thing turns out to be another thing – but the conceptual distance between a shiver and a convulsion is perhaps not great enough. Neither does the juxtaposition have the shock value of Kafka's best juxtapositions – like a tightrope that turns out to be a tripwire. I am intrigued by the father's worry about the charwoman ('If we continue like this we'll soon be having a charwoman in our family'): GPT-3 seems to have zoomed in on the social structure of Kafka's story world here, detecting an uneasy relationship between the family and the charwoman, who is simultaneously deeply involved in the most intimate family secret, and yet necessarily remains outside the charmed family circle due to her lower social position. In this way, the GPT-3 'extension' brings out yet another dimension of Kafka's drama of power relations in a family. And then there is the ending: GPT-3 correctly identifies unexplained, perhaps inexplicable laughter as a native element of Kafka's imagination, but Grete's 'just because' seems off. The tone is all wrong.

But the fact that GPT-3 has not cracked the code of Kafka's tone does not mean that it will forever remain beyond the grasp of artificial intelligence – perhaps not even for very long at all. March 2023 saw the release of GPT-4, which is bigger – meaning trained with a bigger neural network – and more capable than its predecessors. It can, for example, pass the bar exam with a score in the top 10 per cent, as opposed to GPT-3's score in the bottom 10 per cent. And it generates better text, not least because it can correctly explain the idiosyncrasies of English that confounded the earlier versions of the software.

The rise of large language models and generative artificial intelligence puts the question of the function and value of literature front and centre. Would we want to read what ChatGPT writes in the same way that we want to read what Kafka wrote? Stephen Marche's answer in his *New Yorker* article tends towards the negative: according to him, Kafka's *Metamorphosis* 'doesn't need extension. It's perfect. It has survived because the core meaning of its story continues to resonate. Gregor is subject to a miracle that is at once a revelation and a catastrophe. The human entity changes once again, in a way that is both magical and degrading.'

While I share his fascination with Kafka's story, I do not fully agree with Marche's assessment. Tracking down Kafka's readers over the decades all around the world I have seen time and again that the desire to 'extend' his stories into new times, places and contexts, fan fiction-style, plays a central part in the attraction he holds for readers. GPT-3's extension of *The Metamorphosis* has its precursor in Karl Brand's 'Retransformation of Gregor Samsa', written in Prague soon after the publication of Kafka's story. It is not even the first such extension printed in the *New Yorker*. Haruki Murakami's Japanese story of 'Samsa in Love' was published in the very same venue some ten years earlier.

AI is not the first modern technology that came to be associated with Kafka either. Something I did not get to experience in Prague, but could have, had I only travelled there a few years earlier, was the intriguingly titled 'VRwandlung' at the local Goethe-Institut, a German cultural institution with offices all around the world, set up to promote the study of German language and culture. With a name that plays on the German title of Kafka's *Verwandlung*, this virtual-reality experience promises to transform its visitor into Gregor Samsa waking up in his meticulously reproduced room, though only for four minutes. Its creators proudly report that it is the first VR design to recreate the experience of walking around on no fewer than six legs and in this way makes Kafka into a virtual-reality innovator.

The creators of 'VRwandlung' go so far as to identify Kafka as 'the spiritual father of virtual reality'. Perhaps it is not so unexpected: critics have long been fascinated by Kafka's attitude towards modern technologies of his day, as well as those yet to be developed. 'As an enthusiastic cinemagoer and viewer of stereoscopic images, he imagined that one day a two-dimensional image would be fused with spatial effects to create a new, completely illusionary reality', explains Reiner Stach, Kafka's biographer, whose virtual tour accompanies visitors.

Kafka's fiancée Felice Bauer's thoroughly modern job was as a marketer for parlographs – devices that can mechanically record and reproduce sound – manufactured by Carl Lindström AG in Berlin. In one letter about her work, Kafka mused about what would come to be known as the answering machine:

Invent a combination of telephone and Parlograph. This really can't be too difficult. The day after tomorrow, of course, you will tell me that this has already been accomplished successfully. But it really would be of immense importance for the press, news agencies, etc. More difficult, but surely quite possible, would be a combination of gramophone and telephone. More difficult, simply because one can't understand a word the gramophone says, and a Parlograph can't very well ask for clearer pronunciation. A combination of gramophone and telephone would not be of such great universal importance; it would only be a relief to people who, like me, are afraid of the telephone. People like me, however, are equally afraid of the gramophone, so for them there is no help whatever. Here, by the way, is a rather nice idea: a Parlograph goes to the telephone in Berlin, while a gramophone does likewise in Prague, and these two carry on a little conversation with each other. But dearest, the combination of Parlograph and telephone simply must be invented.

This, to me, is Kafka at his best: funny and self-deprecating, he displays an appealing combination of tepid interest in the practical applications of modern technology and an unbounded fascination with wholly absurd but technically possible scenarios, such as two machines sharing an affable chat over the wires stretching across from his Prague to Bauer's Berlin.

As much as I wince going through the promotional materials of 'VRwandlung' online – is it not just an empty gimmick? – I have to concede that Kafka would have probably found the idea enthralling. From Prague, 'VRwandlung' travelled on to fifty other cities, including as far as various Asian countries: India, Pakistan, Bangladesh, Sri Lanka and Taiwan. It was visited – or experienced? – by everybody from Czech schoolchildren to Hollywood actor Orlando Bloom, proudly featured on the website of the Goethe-Institut. For many visitors, it was their first experience with a VR headset of any kind. How curious that for all of them, this new technology – which is only set to gain more popularity in the coming years – will be forever associated with Kafka's literary masterpiece.

How to make sense of this enduring fascination of Kafka for tech companies? Apache Kafka – often just referred to as Kafka – is a type of computer network for storing data, created at LinkedIn in 2011. Asked about the software's name, its creator Jay Kreps explained: 'I thought that since Kafka was a system optimized for writing using a writer's name would make sense. I had taken a lot of lit classes in college and liked Franz Kafka. Plus the name sounded cool for an open source project.' Not unlike the East Asian businesses that use the name Kafka because it sounds pleasing

– short, distinctive, catchy – Kreps was attracted to the 'cool sound' of the name.

But I think more is at stake here. Berthold Franke from the German cultural association that funded 'VRwandlung' explains that the project is 'a perfect coincidence of technology and text. You're transformed by the headset, then you're transformed again in the story.' *The Metamorphosis* is a work that fits the parameters of the technology extremely well, points out a report on the Prague show in *The Economist*: the story plays out in a small space and its protagonist only engages in minimal interactions with others. More broadly, with their transhuman transformations, claustrophobic environments and highly specialised objects whose deeper purpose remains elusive, Kafka's most famous texts, such as *The Metamorphosis* and *The Trial*, clearly speak to our encounters with modern technology, especially when it feels uncanny: exciting and threatening at the same time.

This is also why, after years of investigating Kafka's cultural afterlives around the world, I seem to feel much less exasperation than most of my colleagues at the omnipresence of the term 'Kafkaesque', which, they worry, has emptied the word of any meaning. But that is not the way I look at it. For me, the ubiquity of this term shows that literature matters to us, that it structures our thinking, that it helps us navigate novelty. Analysing its uses, sometimes based on false assumptions – like the claim that Kafka would have been particularly alert to the dangers of AI because he himself was 'failed by systems of power' – is an opportunity to train ourselves to think better, with more nuance and precision.

Kafka the software, Kafka the inventor of virtual reality,

Kafka the critic of artificial intelligence: unlike many of my other favourite classics of European modernism gathering dust in university libraries, the man from Prague seems to have adapted to the age of the cloud remarkably well. But a different kind of search for Kafka in the twenty-first century also continues apace – by decidedly analogue means.

In 1971, Kathi Diamant was a student at the University of Georgia. In a German literature class, her instructor asked if she was related to Dora Diamant, Kafka's last partner. She promised to find out – and even though the answer turned out to be no, her fascination with the couple was not diminished. Kathi Diamant's biography of Dora Diamant was published in 2003, building on the results of the Kafka Project, which she founded a few years earlier as an 'independent international investigation' aiming to 'solve the literary mystery' of Kafka's lost manuscripts. The lost writings include, Kathi Diamant estimates, thirty-five letters and up to twenty notebooks written during the last months of Kafka's life, which he left to Dora Diamant, and which were confiscated from her Berlin apartment by the Gestapo in 1933.

Nearly thirty years since its foundation, the project is still going strong. Perusing its intermittent reports is thrilling. In the early 2000s, three letters penned by Kafka were found in private hands in California, where Kathi Diamant lives – as well as, in an Israeli kibbutz, what appears to be Kafka's hairbrush, brought there by Dora Diamant in 1950. Then, in 2008, the team pivoted: 'We learned that if Kafka's lost writings still exist, they are safely buried among top-secret documents in closed archives in Poland' – deposited there by the German Army in the 1940s. But the search was difficult and the papers were not found. I perk up. A sweet vision unfolds in my mind's eye: a native of Cracow, where Dora Diamant lived as a teenager, now a Kafka expert from Oxford, fluent in English, German and Polish, familiar with the unspoken rules to be followed when dealing with the bureaucrats of my homeland, I fling open the archive doors, reach for a musty cardboard box, and triumphantly pull out a crumbling notebook covered in Kafka's unmistakeable handwriting. My search for Kafka comes full circle: perhaps I even get to bring the long-lost manuscripts to Oxford, pulling off a twenty-first-century version of Malcolm Pasley's feat in the 1960s. I have a killer coda to my book.

But that, reader, does not come to pass – for many reasons, not least of which is that the Kafka Project went on to learn in 2012 that the relevant papers confiscated by the Gestapo had in fact been moved to Moscow, and then in 2013 that they had been returned to East Berlin during the Cold War. They remain in the German Federal Archives today, still uncatalogued. According to the most recent update on the Kafka Project website, at the beginning of 2023 Kathi Diamant travelled to Berlin to meet with the Kafka scholar and editor Hans-Gerd Koch, who continues to petition the German Federal Archives to finance the cataloguing of the documents confiscated by the Gestapo.

Could Kafka's lost last writings really be there? The search continues.

Notes

Prologue

Brod wrote about the 'magic charm' of Kafka's words in his early biography: see Max Brod, *Über Franz Kafka* (Frankfurt am Main: S. Fischer, 1993), my translation. Kafka's letters are quoted from Franz Kafka, *Letters to Friends, Family, and Editors*, trans. Richard and Clara Winston (New York: Schocken, 1977). Kafka's diaries are quoted from Franz Kafka, *Diaries*, trans. Ross Benjamin (New York: Schocken, 2022).

1. Oxford

Fiona McLees published two articles about her work on Kafka's manuscripts, one aimed at other conservators, and one for the general public: 'From Author's Draft to Select Library Holding: The Metamorphosis of Franz Kafka's Manuscripts', in *Works of Art on Parchment and Paper: Interdisciplinary Approaches*, ed. Nataša Golob and Jedert Vodopivec Tomažič (Ljubljana, 2019), pp. 181–90, and 'Kafka's Trail', *Literary Review*, 490 (2020), p. 64. In her talk, McLees quoted from Philip Larkin, 'A Neglected Responsibility: Contemporary Literary Manuscripts', *Encounter*, July 1979, pp. 33–41, and Andrew Motion, 'Such Attics Cleared of Me: Saving Writers' Manuscripts for the Nation', *Times Literary Supplement*, 6 October 2006, pp. 14–15.

The two articles by Malcolm Pasley cited in this chapter are 'Kafka's *Der Process*: What the Manuscript Can Tell Us', *Oxford German Studies*, 18 (1989), 109–18, and 'Franz Kafka MSS: Description and Select Inedita', *Modern Language Review*, 57 (1962), 53–9. The edition of *The Trial* that presents each chapter in a separate booklet is Franz Kafka, *Der Prozess*, ed. Roland Reuß und Peter Staengle (Basel: Stroemfeld, 1997). Other quotes about Kafka's manuscripts in this chapter come from Reiner Stach, *Kafka: The Years of Insight*, trans. Shelley Frisch (Princeton: Princeton University Press, 2015), and Osman Durrani, 'Editions, Translations, Adaptations', in *The Cambridge Companion to Kafka*, ed. Julian Preece (Cambridge: Cambridge University Press, 2002), pp. 206–25. I also cite Ulrich Greiner, 'Kafkas Halbbruder', *Die Zeit*, 41 (1992), and two obituaries of Pasley by T. J. Reed, 'John Malcolm Sabine Pasley, 1926–2004', *Proceedings of the British Academy*, 150 (2007), 149–57, and by Kevin Hilliard, *Daily Telegraph*, 25 March 2004. The story of Kafka's manuscripts' journey to Oxford has also recently been recounted by Carolin Duttlinger in 'Kafka in Oxford', *Oxford German Studies*, 50.4 (2021), 416–27. The price of the manuscript of *The Trial* was reported in *The New York Times* on 17 November 1988: Terry Trucco, 'A Kafka Manuscript Is Sold for $1.98 Million'.

I consulted the following German edition of *Die Verwandlung*: Franz Kafka, *Ein Landarzt und andere Drucke zu Lebzeiten* (Frankfurt am Main: S. Fischer, 2008). I also used the following English translations of the story: Franz Kafka, *The Metamorphosis and Other Stories*, trans. Joyce Crick (Oxford: Oxford University Press, 2009); Franz Kafka, *Metamorphosis and Other Stories*, trans. Michael Hofmann (London: Penguin, 2015); and Franz Kafka, *The Metamorphosis*, trans. Susan Bernofsky (New York: W. W. Norton, 2014).

I quoted from the following reviews and discussions of various adaptations of *The Metamorphosis* in 2020: Seán Williams's podcast 'Kafka in Quarantine' (www.acflondon.org/events/kafka-quarantine-exploratory-podcast); reviews of the Vanishing Point adaptation in the *Guardian* (www.theguardian.com/stage/2020/mar/16/the-metamorphosis-review-tron-theatre-glasgow), the *Herald* (www.heraldscotland.com/arts_ents/18306444.theatre-review-metamorphosis-tron-theatre-glasgow), and the *Stage* (www.thestage.co.uk/reviews/

the-metamorphosis-review-at-tron-theatre-glasgow--horrifyingly-timely-adaptation); a review of Lokstoff!'s adaptation on SWR2 (https://www.swr.de/swr2/buehne/bildergalerie-vorher-nachher-lokstoff-auto-theater-stuttgart-100.html); and an account of Hijinx's adaptation (www.bbc.co.uk/news/av/uk-wales-53870461).

I also quoted from the following accounts of (re)reading *The Metamorphosis* in 2020: articles in the *Opiate* (www.theopiatemagazine.com/2020/04/26/we-are-all-gregor-samsa-now), the *Missouri Review* (www.missourireview.com/from-kafkas-window-an-essay-of-the-covid-19-pandemic-by-jeffrey-condran) and *Medical Humanities* (blogs.bmj.com/medical-humanities/2020/06/23/a-kafkaesque-pandemic). The study of dreams during the pandemic was reported in Colleen Walsh's interview with Deirdre Barrett in the *Harvard Gazette* (news.harvard.edu/gazette/story/2020/05/harvard-researcher-says-dreams-indicative-of-virus-fears). Johannes Türk writes about Kafka's history of tuberculosis and other lung diseases in 'Health and Illness', in *Kafka in Context*, ed. Carolin Duttlinger (Cambridge: Cambridge University Press, 2017), pp. 44–53. Kafka's diary entry is quoted from Franz Kafka, *The Diaries of Franz Kafka*, trans. Ross Benjamin (New York: Schocken, 2022). A lightly adapted translation of the letter to Oskar Baum is quoted from Franz Kafka, *Letters to Friends, Family, and Editors*, trans. Richard and Clara Winston (New York: Schocken, 1977). I also consulted the German original from Franz Kafka, *Briefe 1918–1920*, ed. Hans-Gerd Koch (Frankfurt am Main: S. Fischer, 2013).

Ian McEwan, *The Cockroach* (London: Jonathan Cape, 2019) is the Brexit-themed retelling of Kafka's *The Metamorphosis*. I also quoted from its various reviews, in the *Guardian* (www.theguardian.com/books/2019/sep/12/ian-mcewan-announces-surprise-brexit-satire-the-cockroach and www.theguardian.com/books/2019/oct/07/the-cockroach-ian-mcewan-review), *Evening Standard* (www.standard.co.uk/culture/books/the-cockroach-by-ian-mcewan-review-a4247016.html), *Deutschlandfunk* (www.deutschlandfunk.de/polit-satire-von-ian-mcewan-eine-kakerlake-macht-brexit.700.de.html?dram:article_id=465796), *Pop Matters* (www.popmatters.

com/ian-mcewan-the-cockroach-2642978358.html), *New Statesman* (www.newstatesman.com/%E2%80%8Bian-mcewan-the-cockroach-brexit-kafka-metamorphosis-review). The cover of Kafka's imagined novel *Brexit* can be seen here: twitter.com/thj1961/status/1111539255866806272.

The *Daily Mail* provided its peculiar definition of the term 'Kafkaesque' here: www.dailymail.co.uk/news/article-11130447/Allies-Boris-draw-dossier-legal-advice-case-against-Harriet-Harmans-probe.

2. Berlin

I quoted Kurt Beals's English translation of Siegfried Wolff's letter from Reiner Stach's *Is That Kafka?: 99 Finds* (New York: New Directions, 2016), p. 235. Dawkins's tweet and the responses to it can be seen here: twitter.com/richarddawkins/status/1401239365678997506?lang=en. Rita Felski writes about literature and feelings in her *Uses of Literature* (Oxford: Blackwell, 2008).

The most extensive examination of Kafka's language skills, especially in Czech, can be found in Marek Nekula's *Franz Kafkas Sprachen* (Tübingen: Max Niemeyer, 2003). Some parts of this book have been translated into English by Robert Russell and Carly McLaughlin and included in Nekula's *Franz Kafka and His Prague Contexts* (Prague: Karolinum, 2016). For a readable account of multilingualism in Europe and beyond, see Gaston Dorren's books *Lingo* (London: Profile, 2014) and *Babel* (London: Profile, 2018). For Peter Zusi's thought experiment, see his forthcoming book *Silent Storytellers: Kafka, Prague, Modernism*.

I have taken the details of the design and installation of David Černý's sculpture from the infographic available at www.quadrio.cz/en/franz-kafka-statue.

Contemporary reviews of Kafka's works are collected in *Franz Kafka. Kritik und Rezeption zu seinen Lebzeiten, 1912–1924* (Frankfurt am Main: S. Fischer, 1979). Quotes given here are in my translation. English quotes from Kafka's letters to Felice Bauer are taken from Franz Kafka, *Letters to Felice*, trans. James Stern and Elisabeth Duckworth

(New York: Schocken, 1973). I also consulted the German original: *Briefe an Felice Bauer* (Frankfurt am Main: S. Fischer, 2015). 'Wish to Become a Red Indian' is quoted in Joyce Crick's translation from Franz Kafka, *The Metamorphosis and Other Stories* (Oxford: Oxford University Press, 2009). An example of the *Zürau Aphorisms* is quoted in Willa and Edwin Muir's translation from *The Great Wall of China: Stories and Reflections* (New York: Schocken, 1970). Kasimir Edschmid's background is discussed in his biography by Hermann Schlösser, *Kasimir Edschmid. Expressionist, Reisender, Romancier. Eine Werkbiographie* (Bielefeld: Aisthesis, 2007). Kristin Kopp's book mentioned in this chapter is *Germany's Wild East: Constructing Poland as Colonial Space* (Ann Arbor: University of Michigan Press, 2012).

Kafka's travel diaries are available in German as Franz Kafka, *Reisetagebücher* (Frankfurt am Main: S. Fischer, 2008). Max Brod and Franz Kafka, *Eine Freundschaft. Reiseaufzeichnungen* (Frankfurt am Main: S. Fischer, 1987), includes notes from Kafka's and Brod's travels together. English translations are quoted from Franz Kafka, *The Diaries of Franz Kafka*, trans. Ross Benjamin (New York: Schocken, 2022). Kafka's letter to Brod is quoted from Franz Kafka, *Letters to Friends, Family, and Editors*, trans. Richard and Clara Winston (New York: Schocken, 1977).

More details on what Kafka read can be found in Ritchie Robertson, 'Kafka's Reading', in *Franz Kafka in Context*, ed. Carolin Duttlinger (Cambridge: Cambridge University Press, 2018), pp. 82–90.

The extensive reconstruction of Kafka's day in Zurich can be found in Hartmut Binder's *Mit Kafka in den Süden* (Prague: Vitalis, 2007). Binder's *Kafkas Wien* (Mitterfels: Vitalis, 2013) chronicles Kafka's infrequent visits to Vienna and his other contacts with the city and its people. Hans-Gerd Koch's *Kafka in Berlin* (Berlin: Klaus Wagenbach, 2008) is an excellent guide to Berlin following in Kafka's footsteps.

Dora Diamant's recollections about Kafka's doll story are reprinted in *'Als Kafka mir entgegenkam . . .' Erinnerungen an Franz Kafka*, ed. Hans-Gerd Koch (Berlin: Klaus Wagenbach, 2005). I quote it in my translation. Marthe Robert's book is *Seul, comme Franz Kafka* (Paris: Calmann-Lévy, 1979). Klaus Wagenbach's book is (in Arthur S.

Wensinger's translation) *Franz Kafka: Pictures of a Life* (New York: Pantheon, 1984). Anthony Rudolf wrote and illustrated one version of the story of the doll, *Kafka's Doll* (London: EMH Arts/Eagle Gallery, 2007). Larissa Theule wrote another, illustrated by Rebecca Green: *Kafka and the Doll* (London: Viking, 2021). Two articles, in Dutch and in German, give an overview of various literary versions of the doll book: Niels Bokhove, 'Kafka's poppebrieven zijn geen verzinsel' (kafka-kring.nl/artikelen/kafkas-poppebrieven) and Magali Nieradka-Steiner, 'Von Briefen, die es nicht (mehr) gibt: Franz Kafka und die Puppe' (dspace.ub.uni-siegen.de/bitstream/ubsi/2085/1/Nieradka-Steiner_Briefe_Ded04.pdf). César Aira's essay, 'La muñeca viajera', was published in *El País* on 7 May 2004. Mark Harman's essay about the search for the lost manuscripts is 'Missing Persons: Two Little Riddles about Kafka and Berlin', *New England Review*, 25 (2004). The story of a photograph of Kafka's Berlin house is recounted in Sarah Mondegrin's article 'Kafka in Berlin: Das vergessene Haus', published in *Der Tagesspiegel* on 2 December 2012.

3. Prague

I consulted two guides to Kafka's Prague: Klaus Wagenbach, *Kafkas Prag. Ein Reiselesebuch* (Berlin: Klaus Wagenbach, 2015), and Harald Salfellner, *Franz Kafka und Prag* (Prague: Vitalis, 2003). Both are also available in an English translation. The letter to Oskar Pollak about Prague is quoted from Franz Kafka, *Letters to Friends, Family, and Editors*, trans. Richard and Clara Winston (New York: Schocken, 1977). Kafka's diary entries are quoted from Franz Kafka, *The Diaries of Franz Kafka*, trans. Ross Benjamin (New York: Schocken, 2022). The translation from Hrabal's story about Mr Kafka comes from Bohumil Hrabal, *Mr. Kafka and Other Tales*, trans. Paul Wilson (London: Vintage, 2016). I also consulted an earlier translation: Bohumil Hrabal, 'The Kafkorium', trans. W. L. Solberg, in *New Writing of East Europe*, ed. George Gömöri and Charles Newman (Chicago: Quadrangle Books, 1968), pp. 179–89. I took the information about the World of Franz Kafka from its website: www.franzkafkaworld.com/en.

Notes

An English translation of Karl Brand's story is appended to Franz Kafka, *The Metamorphosis as well as The Retransformation of Gregor Samsa*, trans. Karen Reppin (Prague: Vitalis, 2020). An English translation of *A Country Doctor*, a collection of stories Kafka wrote on Zlatá ulička, can be found in *A Hunger Artist and Other Stories*, trans. Joyce Crick (Oxford: Oxford University Press, 2012).

The jackdaw on the business stationery of Kafka's father's store is described in the first chapter of Max Brod's biography, *Über Franz Kafka* (Frankfurt am Main: S. Fischer, 1993), p. 11, and can be seen in Klaus Wagenbach, *Franz Kafka. Bilder aus seinem Leben* (Berlin: Klaus Wagenbach, 2008), p. 40 – on both types of tree branches. Kafka's signature and ink drawings can be seen on the covers of two recent German editions of his works published by Fischer.

Jiří Votruba explains his motivations for designing his famous Kafka graphic in an interview with Brian Kenety, 'Graphic (But Not By) Design – Jiří Votruba', *Radio Prague International*, 11 March 2005 (english.radio.cz/graphic-not-design-jiri-votruba-8626137). The book Votruba refers to is presumably Hans-Gerd Koch (ed.), *'Als Kafka mir entgegenkam . . .' Erinnerungen an Franz Kafka*, (Berlin: Klaus Wagenbach, 2005). More information about Votruba's career is available in an interview with Ian Willoughby, 'Jiří Votruba – Artist Whose Work Helps Form Visitors' Image of Prague', *Radio Prague International*, 16 October 2013 (english.radio.cz/jiri-votruba-artist-whose-work-helps-form-visitors-image-prague-8545000).

Veronika Tuckerova presented the results of her research in her doctoral dissertation, 'Reading Kafka in Prague: The Reception of Franz Kafka between the East and the West during the Cold War', submitted at Columbia University in 2012. Jean-Paul Sartre, Ernst Fischer and Antonín Novotný are quoted in Tuckerova's dissertation; I supplemented the English translation of Fischer's quote and lightly modified her translations of Sartre and Novotný. Iakov Elsberg is quoted in Emily Tall, 'Who's Afraid of Franz Kafka? Kafka Criticism in the Soviet Union', *Slavic Review*, 35.3 (1976), 484–503, p. 485. My discussion of the Soviet reception of Thomas Mann can be found in Karolina Watroba, *Mann's Magic Mountain: World Literature and*

Closer Reading (Oxford: Oxford University Press, 2022).

Paul Wilson's translation of Havel's speech 'On Kafka' was published in the *New York Review of Books*, 27 September 1990, and can be accessed online: www.nybooks.com/articles/1990/09/27/on-kafka. Jaroslav Róna's speech about his statue of Kafka can be read here: www.ourbeautifulprague.com/franz-kafka-jaroslav-rona. More information can be found in two interviews with the sculptor: Pavla Horáková, 'Eighty Years After His Death, Franz Kafka Finally Has a Statue in Prague', *Radio Prague International*, 1 September 2004 (english.radio.cz/eighty-years-after-his-death-franz-kafka-finally-has-a-statue-prague-8082061), and Jan Richter, 'Sculptor Jaroslav Róna on Kafka, America, and Life in Prague', *Radio Prague International*, 27 April 2009 (english.radio.cz/sculptor-jaroslav-rona-kafka-america-and-life-prague-8585256). Tania and James Stern's translation of 'Description of a Struggle' comes from a collection of the same title (New York: Schocken, 1958).

Friedrich Thieberger's memory of Kafka at the window is taken from *'Als Kafka mir entgegenkam . . .' Erinnerungen an Franz Kafka*, pp. 134–35. Kafka's CV and job application can be seen on the website of the Assicurazioni Generali Corporate Heritage & Historical Archive: heritage.generali.com/en/story-of-a-special-clerk-franz-kafka-at-generali. His office writings were edited by Klaus Hermsdorf and Benno Wagner and published in German as *Amtliche Schriften* (Frankfurt am Main: S. Fischer, 2004). A selection is available in English: *The Office Writings*, trans. Eric Patton and Ruth Heim (Princeton: Princeton University Press, 2009). Adrian McKinty described his stay at the Franz Kafka Suite in 'On Literary Osmosis and the Perils of Trying to Write in Famous Places', *Literary Hub*, 21 November 2017 (lithub.com/adrian-mckinty-tries-to-get-some-writing-done-in-kafkas-old-office). Elana Wolff described her search for Kafka's hotel in Berlin in 'After Kafka in Berlin', *Eclectica Magazine*, Jan/Feb 2020 (www.eclectica.org/v24n1/wolff.html).

Information about the history of Café Louvre and Café Slavia can be found here: www.cafelouvre.cz/en/history and www.cafeslavia.cz/en/about-cafe. Baum's recollection of Kafka's sketch about the invention of the coffeehouse can be found in 'Als Kafka mir entgegenkam . . .' *Erinnerungen an Franz Kafka*, p. 75. The English translation is taken from Reiner Stach, *Kafka: The Early Years*, trans. Shelley Frisch (Princeton: Princeton University Press, 2017), p. 335.

English quotations from *The Judgement* are from Franz Kafka, *The Metamorphosis and Other Stories*, trans. Joyce Crick (Oxford: Oxford University Press, 2009). I also consulted the German original of *Das Urteil*, in Franz Kafka, *Ein Landarzt und andere Drucke zu Lebzeiten* (Frankfurt am Main: S. Fischer, 2008). The letter to his father is quoted from Franz Kafka, *The Sons*, trans. Ernst Kaiser and Eithne Wilkins (New York: Schocken, 1989). Ten interpretations of the story introducing ten schools of literary theory are included in Oliver Jahraus and Stefan Neuhaus (eds.), *Kafkas* Urteil *und die Literaturtheorie. Zehn Modellanalysen* (Stuttgart: Reclam, 2002). The definition of 'implied readers' comes from Andrew Bennett (ed.), *Readers and Reading* (Abingdon: Routledge, 2013), p. 236. For an accessible introduction to the theory of literary reception, see Ika Willis, *Reception* (Abingdon: Routledge, 2018). The quotation from Kafka's novel set in America comes from Franz Kafka, *The Man who Disappeared (America)*, trans. Ritchie Robertson (Oxford: Oxford University Press, 2012).

The most extensive examination of Kafka's language skills, especially in Czech, can be found in Marek Nekula's *Franz Kafkas Sprachen* (Tübingen: Max Niemeyer, 2003). Some parts of this book have been translated into English by Robert Russell and Carly McLaughlin and included in Nekula's *Franz Kafka and His Prague Contexts* (Prague: Karolinum, 2016). Joyce Crick's translations of both 'Odradek, or Cares of a Householder' and 'Before the Law' can be found in Franz Kafka, *A Hunger Artist and Other Stories*. Kafka's references to Božena Němcová are discussed in Nekula's book, as well as in Hans Dieter Zimmermann, 'Franz Kafka liest Božena Němcová', *Brücken*, 15 (2007), 181–92, and Peter Zusi, 'Czech Language and Literature', in *Kafka in Context*, ed. Carolin Duttlinger (Cambridge: Cambridge University Press, 2017), pp. 159–66. The English translation of 'A Tale Without End' is taken from Božena Němcová, *The Disobedient Kids and Other Czecho-Slovak Fairy Tales*, trans. William

H. Tolman and V. Smetánka (Prague: B. Kočí, 1921). I also consulted
the Czech original in Božena Němcová, *Národní báchorky a pověsti*
(Prague: I. L. Kolber, 1877).

On Ruth Bondy and the grave notes kept at the National Library
of Israel, see Hagit Zimroni, 'On Pilgrimage to Franz Kafka', 9 May
2018 (blog.nli.org.il/en/kafka_pilgrimage). Chaim Kočí is quoted in
Bob Asher, 'Jižní Koreu ohromilo dílo Franze Kafky. Nadšení fanoušci
cestují přes půl světa k jeho hrobu v Praze', *PrahaIN*, 22 January 2023
(www.prahain.cz/zivot-ve-meste/jizni-koreu-ohromilo-dilo-fran-10778.
html).

Some ideas from this chapter are also discussed in Katrin Kohl and
Karolina Watroba, 'Kafka's Global Afterlives', in *Kafka: Making of an
Icon*, ed. Ritchie Robertson (Oxford: Bodleian, forthcoming).

4. *Jerusalem*

Benjamin Balint wrote about the Jerusalem trials in his book *Kafka's
Last Trial: The Case of a Literary Legacy* (London: Pan Macmillan,
2018). Judith Butler's article 'Who Owns Kafka?' was published on 3
March 2011 in the *London Review of Books* (www.lrb.co.uk/the-paper/
v33/no5/judith-butler/who-owns-kafka). Max Brod wrote on Kafka's
yearning for community in 'Unsere Literaten und die Gemeinschaft',
first published in *Der Jude* in 1916; it is reproduced in *Franz Kafka.
Kritik und Rezeption zu seinen Lebzeiten, 1912–1924* (Frankfurt am
Main: S. Fischer, 1979). Dan Miron wrote about Kafka in the context
of Jewish literatures in *From Continuity to Contiguity: Toward a New
Jewish Literary Thinking* (Stanford: Stanford University Press, 2010).

The two articles by Iris Bruce I discuss in this chapter are 'What
if Franz Kafka Had Immigrated to Palestine?', in *What Ifs of Jewish
History: From Abraham to Zionism*, ed. Gavriel D. Rosenfeld
(Cambridge: Cambridge University Press, 2016), and 'Kafka's Journey
into the Future: Crossing Borders into Israeli/Palestinian Worlds',
in *Kafka for the Twenty-First Century*, eds. Stanley Corngold and
Ruth V. Gross (Rochester, NY: Boydell & Brewer, 2011). Atef Botros
al-Attar wrote *Kafka. Ein jüdischer Schriftsteller aus arabischer Sicht*

(Wiesbaden: Reichert Verlag, 2009). A summary of his research in English is available here: www.dohainstitute.org/en/Events/Pages/Franz-kafka-and-Palestine.aspx. Jens Hanssen's article is 'Kafka and Arabs', *Critical Inquiry*, 39.1 (2012), 167–97, and quotations from Malek's novel are taken from it. Kafka's diary entry about the story is quoted from Franz Kafka, *The Diaries of Franz Kafka*, trans. Ross Benjamin (New York: Schocken, 2022). I also consulted the German edition published as part of S. Fischer's *Kritische Ausgabe*. Ritchie Robertson's *Kafka: Judaism, Politics, and Literature* (Oxford, 1987) is an important study of Kafka's relationship to Judaism and Jewishness.

Remigiusz Grzela's book is only available in Polish: *Bagaże Franza K., czyli podróż, której nigdy nie było* (Warsaw: Instytut Wydawniczy Latarnik, 2004). Information about Michał Walczak's *Circus Kafka*, the adaptation of Grzela's book for Teatr Żydowski im. Estery Rachel i Idy Kamińskich, can be accessed here: www.teatr-zydowski.art.pl/spektakle/circus-kafka.

Jeffrey Shandler's book is *Yiddish: Biography of a Language* (Oxford: Oxford University Press, 2020). Lightly adapted English quotations from Kafka's lecture on the Yiddish language are taken from Franz Kafka, *Dearest Father: Stories and Other Writings*, trans. Ernst Kaiser and Eithne Wilkins (New York: Schocken, 1954). I also consulted the German version included in S. Fischer's *Kritische Ausgabe*. Milica Bakić-Hayden wrote of 'nesting Orientalisms' in 'Nesting Orientalisms: The Case of Former Yugoslavia', *Slavic Review*, vol. 54.4 (1995), pp. 917–31.

A list and description of Kafka manuscripts in the Bodleian Library, including the Hebrew notebooks, can be found here: archives.bodleian.ox.ac.uk/repositories/2/resources/12214. Andreas Kilcher discussed the drawing of the 'guardian of the threshold' in *Franz Kafka: The Drawings*, trans. Kurt Beals (New Haven: Yale University Press, 2022). Puah Ben-Tovim's memories of Kafka are included in *'Als Kafka mir entgegenkam . . .' Erinnerungen an Franz Kafka*, ed. Hans-Gerd Koch (Berlin: Klaus Wagenbach, 2005). The English translation of Kafka's letter to her is taken from Mark Nekula, *Franz Kafka and His Prague Contexts*, trans. Robert Russell and Carly McLaughlin (Prague:

Karolinum, 2016). A linguistic analysis of this letter, including the
mistakes Kafka makes, can be found in David Suchoff's article 'Franz
Kafka, Hebrew Writer: The Vaudeville of Linguistic Origins', in *Nexus
1: Essays in German Jewish Studies*, ed. William Collins Donahue
and Martha B. Helfer (Rochester, NY: Boydell & Brewer, 2011),
and his book *Kafka's Jewish Languages: The Hidden Openness of
Tradition* (Philadelphia: University of Pennsylvania Press, 2012). Alfred
Bodenheimer, the editor of the forthcoming edition of Kafka's Hebrew
writings, published two articles about them: 'A Sign of Sickness and a
Symbol of Health: Kafka's Hebrew Notebooks', in *Kafka, Zionism,
and Beyond*, ed. Mark H. Gelber (Tübingen: Max Niemeyer, 2004),
and 'Kafkas Hebräischstudien. Gedanken zur Magie der Mitte und zur
Fragmentierung sprachlichen Denkens', in *Schrift und Zeit in Franz
Kafkas Oktavheften*, eds. Caspar Battegay, Felix Christen and Wolfram
Groddeck (Göttingen: Wallstein, 2010).

Information about Ruth Kanner's play *The Hebrew Notebook* can
be found here: www.ruthkanner.com/en/show/1418. I am grateful to
Shira Yovel, the managing director of the Ruth Kanner Theatre Group,
for arranging a screening of the play for me. Freddie Rokem wrote about
it in two articles: 'The Hebrew Notebook – And Other Stories by Franz
Kafka. A Work of "Speech Theatre" by the Ruth Kanner Theatre Group',
in *Thewis* (2017): www.theater-wissenschaft.de/artikel-the-hebrew-
notebook-and-other-stories-by-franz-kafka, and 'Before the Hebrew
Notebook: Kafka's Words and Gestures in Translation', in *The
German–Hebrew Dialogue: Studies of Encounter and Exchange*, eds.
Amir Eshel and Rachel Seelig (Berlin: De Gruyter, 2018).

Sander Gilman's book is *Franz Kafka, The Jewish Patient* (New
York: Routledge, 1995). Kafka's apartment at the time of writing 'Great
Noise' and *The Metamorphosis* is described in Harald Salfellner, *Franz
Kafka und Prag* (Prague: Vitalis, 2003). The English translation of
'Great Noise' is quoted from Franz Kafka, *The Diaries of Franz Kafka*,
trans. Ross Benjamin (New York: Schocken, 2022). Quotations from
The Trial are taken from the following edition: Franz Kafka, *The Trial*,
trans. Mike Mitchell (Oxford: Oxford University Press, 2009). I also
consulted the German version: Franz Kafka, *Der Proceß. Roman in der*

Fassung der Handschrift (Frankfurt am Main: S. Fischer, 2017).

On the reception of Kafka in France, see John T. Hamilton, *France/Kafka: An Author in Theory* (New York: Bloomsbury, 2023). Kafka's newspaper report from Italy is 'Aeroplanes in Brescia', in Franz Kafka, *Metamorphosis and Other Stories*, trans. Michael Hofmann (London: Penguin, 2020). On the reception of Kafka in Italy, see Saskia Elizabeth Ziolkowski, *Kafka's Italian Progeny* (Toronto: University of Toronto Press, 2020). On the Muirs, as well as some of Kafka's other translators, including Milena Jesenská, see Michelle Woods, *Kafka Translated: How Translators Have Shaped our Reading of Kafka* (New York: Bloomsbury, 2014). On Kafka and Borges, see Sarah Roger, *Borges and Kafka: Sons and Writers* (Oxford: Oxford University Press, 2017), and Alberto Manguel, 'Borges Reads Kafka', *Variaciones Borges*, 46 (2018), 61–76. The quote from 'The Lottery in Babylon' comes from Jorge Luis Borges, *Collected Fictions*, trans. Andrew Hurley (New York: Penguin, 1998), pp. 101–6.

Seloua Luste Boulbina's book is *Kafka's Monkey and Other Phantoms of Africa*, trans. Laura Hengehold (Bloomington, Indiana: Indiana University Press, 2019). Mark Christian Thompson commented on his book, *Kafka's Blues: Figurations of Racial Blackness in the Construction of an Aesthetic* (Evanston, Illinois: Northwestern University Press, 2016), in an interview with Bret McCabe: hub.jhu. edu/magazine/2017/summer/mark-christian-thompson-new-reading-of-kafka. A. Igoni Barrett's novel is *Blackass* (London: Chatto & Windus, 2015). An excerpt from Phoebe Bay Carter's translation of Mohammed Said Hjiouij's *Kafka in Tangier* was published by *ArabLit Quarterly*: arablit.org/2021/12/20/new-an-excerpt-of-mohammed-said-hjiouijs-kafka-in-tangier. Matéi Visniec's *Mr K Released* was published in Jozefina Komporaly's translation by Seagull in 2020. Information on Kafka's reception in India was taken from Faizal Khan's article published on the website of the Goethe-Institut in 2019: www.goethe. de/ins/bd/en/kul/art/vrw/21678297.html. Information on the Unfolding Kafka Festival was taken from its website: www.unfoldingkafkafestival. com.

5. Seoul

In romanisations of Korean, Chinese and Japanese names, I followed conventions established in English-language publications for each individual author.

Haruki Murakami's 'Samsa in Love', trans. Ted Goossen, was published in the *New Yorker* on 21 October 2013: www.newyorker.com/magazine/2013/10/28/samsa-in-love. Elif Batuman's tongue-in-cheek book recommendation can be found here: content.time.com/time/specials/packages/article/0,28804,2000447_2000458_2000476,00.html.

Letters to Felice Bauer are quoted from Franz Kafka, *Letters to Felice*, trans. James Stern and Elisabeth Duckworth (New York: Schocken, 1973). On Kafka and China, see Rolf J. Goebel, *Constructing China: Kafka's Orientalist Discourse* (Columbia: Camden House, 1997), and Yanbing Zeng, *Franz Kafka and Chinese Culture*, trans. Yuan Li (Singapore: Palgrave Macmillan, 2022). Can Xue spoke about Kafka in an interview with Dylan Suher, translated by Joan Hua, in *Asymptote*: www.asymptotejournal.com/interview/an-interview-with-can-xue/.

Yoko Tawada's book is quoted in Susan Bernofsky's translation: *Memoirs of a Polar Bear* (London: Portobello, 2017). The German version has a different title: *Etüden im Schnee* ('Études in the Snow'). 'Josefine, the Singer or The Mouse-People' is quoted from Franz Kafka, *A Hunger Artist and Other Stories*, trans. Joyce Crick (Oxford: Oxford University Press, 2012). I also consulted the German version: 'Josefine, die Sängerin oder Das Volk der Mäuse', in Franz Kafka, *Ein Landarzt und andere Drucke zu Lebzeiten* (Frankfurt am Main: S. Fischer, 2008). On the structure of Kafka's paradoxes, see Gerhard Neumann, 'Umkehrung und Ablenkung: Franz Kafkas "Gleitendes Paradox"', *Deutsche Vierteljahrsschrift für Literaturwissenschaft und Geistesgeschichte*, 42 (1968), 702–44. Marcel Duchamp's dictum is quoted in Louis Aragon et al. (eds.), *Dictionnaire abrégé du surréalisme* (Paris: J. Corti, 1969), p. 23. Tawada commented on Kafka's significance for her own work, and his popularity in East Asia, in an interview with Claire Horst in 2009: heimatkunde.boell.de/

de/2009/02/18/fremd-sein-ist-eine-kunst-interview-mit-yoko-tawada. The bibliography of secondary literature on Kafka mentioned in this chapter is Maria Luise Caputo-Mayr and Julius M. Herz (eds.), *Franz Kafka. Internationale Bibliographie der Primär- und Sekundärliteratur / International Bibliography of Primary and Secondary Literature* (Munich: Saur, 2000), p. xxii.

'A Message from the Emperor' is quoted from Franz Kafka, *A Hunger Artist and Other Stories* (Oxford: Oxford University Press, 2012), translation © Joyce Crick 2012. Reproduced with permission of the Licensor through PLSclear. I also consulted the German version: 'Eine kaiserliche Botschaft' in Franz Kafka, *Ein Landarzt und andere Drucke zu Lebzeiten* (Frankfurt am Main: S. Fischer, 2008). An outline of Kafka's reception in Korea by Lee Yu-sun and Mok Seong-sook, 'Kafka in Korea', published in 2014 as part of Ekkehard W. Haring's *Kafka-Atlas*, is available here (in German): www.kafka-atlas.org/src/docs/beitraege/7a620_Kafka%20in%20Korea.pdf. Oh Kyu-won's poem in Shyun J. Ahn's translation is available here: ahntranslation.com/2017/06/24/franz-kafka-oh-kyu-won/. English translation reproduced with permission from Shyun J. Ahn. Gu Byeong-mo's *The Old Woman with the Knife* in Chi-Young Kim's translation was published by Canongate in 2022.

On the *OED* 'K-update', see here: oed.com/discover/daebak-a-k-update. On literature and the Korean wave, see Jenny Wang Medina, 'From Tradition to Brand: The Making of "Global" Korean Culture in Millennial South Korea', PhD thesis, Columbia University, 2015, as well as Wang Medina, 'At the Gates of Babel: The Globalization of Korean Literature as World Literature', *Acta Koreana*, 21.2 (2018), 395–422, and Wang Medina, 'Global Korea and World Literature', in Heekyoung Cho (ed.), *The Routledge Companion to Korean Literature* (Abingdon: Routledge, 2022). On the mission and budget of the Literature Translation Institute of Korea, see www.ltikorea.or.kr/en/contents/about_inst_1/view.do and www.ltikorea.or.kr/upload/bizyearbook/20220407173109982405.pdf. The adoption of the term 'K-lit' by the South Korean Ministry of Culture, Sports and Tourism is discussed by Bo-Seon Shim in 'A "K" To Bridge Korea and the

World: The State-Led Formulation of K-Lit and Its Contradictions', *International Journal of Asian Studies*, 20.1 (2023), 57–76. A summary of the Nielsen Book Scan report on sales of translated fiction in 2015 can be found here: www.thebookseller.com/news/sales-translated-fic-grow-96-328500. Kyung-Sook Shin, whose novel *Please Look After Mom* in Chi-Young Kim's translation was published by Knopf in 2011, spoke about Kafka here: www.bananawriters.com/kyungsookshin.

Cho Nam-joo's *Kim Jiyoung, Born 1982* in Jamie Chang's translation was published by Scribner in 2020 and reviewed by Euny Hong in *The New York Times*: www.nytimes.com/2020/04/14/books/review/kim-jiyoung-born-1982-cho-nam-joo.html. On South Korea's gender wage gap and low fertility rate, see www.oecd.org/country/korea/thematic-focus/gender-equality-korea-has-come-a-long-way-but-there-is-more-work-to-do-8bb81613 and www.theguardian.com/world/2023/feb/22/south-koreas-birthrate-sinks-to-fresh-record-low-as-population-crisis-deepens, respectively.

In the UK, Han Kang's *The Vegetarian* in Deborah Smith's translation was published by Portobello in 2015. It has been described as 'Kafkaesque' or compared to Kafka's works by its US publisher (www.penguinrandomhouse.com/books/250333/the-vegetarian-by-han-kang), Man Booker International judge Boyd Tonkin (www.theguardian.com/books/booksblog/2016/may/18/kafkaesque-a-word-so-overused-it-has-lost-all-meaning), *New York Times* reviewer Porochista Khakpour (www.nytimes.com/2016/02/07/books/review/the-vegetarian-by-han-kang.html), the Oprah Network reviewer Dotun Akintoye (www.oprah.com/book/translated-books-the-vegetarian?editors_pick_id=61882), and Lonely Planet's *Seoul* by Thomas O'Malley and Phillip Tang, p. 204, among others. Sabine Peschel asked Han Kang about Kafka in an interview titled 'Korea's Kafka?' published by *Deutsche Welle* on 9 December 2016: www.dw.com/en/koreas-kafka-man-booker-winner-han-kang-on-why-she-turns-a-woman-into-a-plant/a-19543017. Dominic O'Key commented on the presentation of *The Vegetarian* as a 'grandchild' of Kafka's work in 'Han Kang's *The Vegetarian* and the International Booker Prize: Reading With and Against World Literary Prestige', *Textual*

Practice, 36.8 (2022), 1262–88. Sooyun Yum commented on the reception of *The Vegetarian* in an interview with Lee Yew Leong in *Asymptote*: www.asymptotejournal.com/special-feature/an-interview-with-sooyun-yum-literature-translation-institute-of-korea/.

Kim Young-ha spoke about his admiration for Kafka here: ch.yes24.com/Article/View/12951; his TED Talk is available here: www.ted.com/talks/young_ha_kim_be_an_artist_right_now/transcript.

On the 'Kafka legend' in Japanese publishing, see Takako Fujita, 'Die Verwandlung der Literatur durch Übersetzung. Glücksfall und Unglücksfall', in Ernest W. B. Hess-Lüttich and Joachim Warmbold (eds.), *Empathie und Distanz. Zur Bedeutung der Übersetzung aktueller Literatur im interkulturellen Dialog* (Frankfurt am Main: Peter Lang, 2009), pp. 119–28 (p. 121). Merriam-Webster reported on the surge in searches for the word 'Kafkaesque' here: www.merriam-webster.com/news-trend-watch/kafkaesque-2016-05-17.

Most quotations from Bae Suah's novella are taken from Bae Suah, *Milena, Milena, Ecstatic*, trans. Deborah Smith (Norwich: Strangers Press, 2019). I also consulted the Korean version: *Millena, Millena, Hwangholhan* (Seoul: Theoria, 2016). I chose to include quotations from Kafka's letters to Jesenská that appear in Bae's novella in a lightly adapted translation taken from Franz Kafka, *Letters to Milena*, trans. Philip Boehm (New York: Schocken, 1990), rather than in Deborah Smith's translation. As the letters travelled across multiple languages, a couple of mistakes, not present in the Korean, seem to have crept into Smith's English: she dates the letter from 14 July as 17 July, and translates the Czech 'i' ('and') as 'I'.

Erica Nardozzi reported on Kafka on TikTok for the *Daily Mail* on 10 February 2023: www.dailymail.co.uk/femail/article-11737477/Franz-Kafka-unlikely-HEARTTHROB-TikTok. Bae's comments on her female protagonists, shamanism and Mongolia come from an interview in the *White Review* from March 2017, trans. Deborah Smith: www.thewhitereview.org/feature/interview-bae-suah. Jesenská's diagnosis is quoted in Reiner Stach, *Kafka: The Years of Insight*, trans. Shelley Frisch (Princeton: Princeton University Press, 2015), p. 325. On Kafka's letters, see Julian Preece, 'The Letters and Diaries', in *The Cambridge*

Companion to Franz Kafka, ed. Preece (Cambridge: Cambridge University Press, 2002), pp. 111–30. On Bauer's letters, see Hans-Gerd Koch's editorial afterword in *Briefe an Felice Bauer* (Frankfurt am Main: S. Fischer, 2015).

Coda

Mark Coeckelbergh's book is *The Political Philosophy of AI* (Cambridge: Polity, 2022). Max Tegmark's book is *Life 3.0: Being Human in the Age of Artificial Intelligence* (London: Allen Lane, 2017). Stephen Cave's article was published in the *Guardian* on 4 January 2019: www.theguardian.com/commentisfree/2019/jan/04/future-democratise-ai-artificial-intelligence-power.

Stephen Marche's article on his experiments with Sudowrite was published in the *New Yorker* on 30 April 2021: www.newyorker.com/culture/cultural-comment/the-computers-are-getting-better-at-writing. OpenAI describes GPT-4 and its capabilities, as compared with GPT-3, here: openai.com/research/gpt-4. Kafka's diary entry is quoted from Franz Kafka, *The Diaries of Franz Kafka*, trans. Ross Benjamin (New York: Schocken, 2022).

On 'VRwandlung', see Tomáš Moravec, 'Kafka ve virtuální realitě', www.goethe.de/ins/cz/cs/kul/mag/21150235.html, translated by Faith Ann Gibson here: www.goethe.de/en/uun/pub/akt/g18/21150235.html. Letters to Felice Bauer are quoted from Franz Kafka, *Letters to Felice*, trans. James Stern and Elisabeth Duckworth (New York: Schocken, 1973). Jay Kreps, the creator of Apache Kafka, answered the question 'What is the relation between Kafka, the writer, and Apache Kafka, the distributed messaging system?' on Quora.com: www.quora.com/What-is-the-relation-between-Kafka-the-writer-and-Apache-Kafka-the-distributed-messaging-system/answer/Jay-Kreps. Berthold Franke is quoted in the *Economist*'s report on 'VRwandlung', 'Is Literature Next in Line for Virtual-reality Treatment?' from 8 March 2018: www.economist.com/books-and-arts/2018/03/08/is-literature-next-in-line-for-virtual-reality-treatment.

Kathi Diamant's biography of Dora Diamant is *Kafka's Last Love:*

The Mystery of Dora Diamant (London: Secker & Warburg, 2003). Information about the Kafka Project, including its intermittent reports, can be found here: kafka.sdsu.edu.

While every effort has been made to contact the relevant copyright holders for quoted text, the editor and publishers would be grateful for information where they have been unable to trace them, and would be glad to make amendments in further editions.

Acknowledgements

I would like to thank all the many people – students, colleagues, friends, acquaintances and occasionally strangers – with whom I have had many interesting conversations about Kafka over the years.

I am also indebted to Conor Brennan, Niamh Burns, Rajendra Chitnis, Carolin Duttlinger, Rita Felski, Adriana X. Jacobs, Haneul Lee, Julia Peck, Jiyoung Shin, and Tanvi Solanki who all read parts of the manuscript and offered useful feedback and invaluable encouragement, and in particular Ritchie Robertson, who read the whole manuscript and whose kind interest in my ideas has been a great source of support.

I am most grateful to my agent, Chris Wellbelove, and his team at Aitken Alexander Associates, as well as my editor, Cecily Gayford, and her team at Profile Books. It has been a pleasure working with and learning from you.

I came up with the idea for this book, wrote it, and saw it through to publication during a five-year-long fellowship at All Souls College. It is difficult to imagine a more inspiring and supportive community in which to undertake a project like this. I would also like to acknowledge support from the British Academy, whose 2022–2023 Talent Development Award helped me to carry out the research underpinning the discussion of Kafka's reception in Korea in this book.

As always, the biggest thank you goes to Kacper Kowalczyk: without you I would have never attempted, let alone finished this book.

Index

Index

Index

reception theory 178
Reed, Jim 22
'A Report to an Academy'
    163
'The Retransformation of
    Gregor Samsa' 83–4, 85,
    215
Reversalism 35–6
Rilke, Rainer Maria 83
Robert, Marthe 73
Robson, Leo 37
Rokem, Freddie 148, 150
Romania 165
Róna, Jaroslav 95–6
Roth, Philip 162
Royal Ballet 29–30
Rudolf, Anthony 72

S
S. Fischer Verlag 83, 147
Said, Edward 142
'Samsa in Love' 167–8
sanatorium 65–6, 67–8
Sartre, Jean-Paul 89, 161
Sauer, August 62
Schiller, Friedrich 61–2, 64
Schmid, Eduard see Edschmid,
    Kasimir
Schocken, Salman 162
Seoul 127–8, 167–208
Sexton, David 36
Seyama, Yoko 166
Shakespeare a Synové 81
shamanism 207, 208
Shandler, Jeffrey 137–8

Sheldonian Theatre 11–12
Shih, Shu-mei 4
Shin, Kyung-Sook 190
'The Silence of Insects' 166
Singh, Rosy 165
Slavdom 59–60, 62, 79
Slavic House 119
Slavonic languages 120–1
Smith, Deborah 188, 191, 196,
    197, 198–9, 202
Solberg, W. L. 81
Song Suk-jae 180
South America 163
South Korea 127–8, 167–208
souvenirs 85, 87, 96, 98, 116–17
Soviet Russia 79, 88–9, 152
Spanish flu 31, 32–3
Stach, Reiner 20, 32–3, 216
Steglitz 75–6
Steiner, Marianne 21
Stephens, Christopher John 36
'The Stoker' 200
Strindberg, August 6, 94
Sudowrite 210–14
Switzerland 60, 65–6, 68
    see also Zurich
Szokoll, Juliane 'Hansi' 73

T
'A Tale Without End' 122–5
Tawada, Yoko 170–4, 176, 178
Tegmark, Max 209
Theule, Larissa 74
Thompson, Mark Christian 164
Tonkin, Boyd 194